American Prisoner

Above the Cage

A prisoner's personal
self-help and
rehabilitation guide

D. Razor Babb

Copyright © 2015 D. Razor Babb

All rights reserved.

ISBN: 0692624371
ISBN-13: 978-0692524374

Published by LWL Enterprises, Inc.

D. Razor Babb

Caged Bird
By Maya Angelou

A free bird leaps
on the back of the wind
and floats downstream
till the current ends
and dips his wing
in the orange sun rays
and dares to claim the sky.

But a bird that stalks
down his narrow cage can seldom see through
his bars of rage
his wings are clipped and
his feet are tied
so he opens his throat to sing.

The caged bird sings
with a fearful trill
of things unknown
but longed for still
and his tune is heard
on the distant hill
for the caged bird
sings of freedom.

The free bird thinks of another breeze
and the trade winds soft through the sighing trees
and the fat worms waiting on a dawn bright lawn
and he names the sky his own.

But a caged bird stands on a grave of dreams
his shadow shouts on a nightmare scream
his wings are clipped and his feet are tied
so he opens his throat to sing.

The caged bird sings
with a fearful trill
of things unknown but longed for still
and his tune is heard
on the distant hill
for the caged bird
sings of freedom.

American Prisoner

Dedication

In Brian Stevenson's memoir <u>Just Mercy</u> he says, "Each of us is more than the worst thing we've ever done." I know this to be true. The penitentiaries are full of men and women who have done terrible things, who have committed many sins and made many mistakes. The lives of all people are dark with many sins. If we strive to improve and take each step forward with noble intent, we may not only better our own lives but the lives of those around us. In this way we help one another find our way out of the darkness.

<u>American Prisoner</u> is dedicated to all those souls seeking the light.

Acknowledgements

With sincere appreciation and gratitude, I thank the following individuals for their unselfish and earnest assistance with <u>American Prisoner</u>.

Keith Kakugawa, Woodrow Fitzhugh, Dr. Jude Lawcen, Ron Gregg, Bob Barber, and the super-human efforts of Leah Ward-Lee for publishing under such extreme circumstances and extraordinary deadline demands.

Devah Pager for her research and for the insightful book, <u>Marked,</u> from which the incarceration statistics were drawn.

There are many others who have played a part in <u>American Prisoner</u>, filtering in and out of my life as the universe commands, a part of the conspiracy to accomplish what I hope will be deemed a worthwhile effort. To all those divine souls here and beyond, love, peace, light, freedom.

D. Razor Babb

Razor Babb doesn't tell us what an American prisoner is; we arrive at the discovery through a prism of the transpersonal journey.

– Woodrow Fitzhugh

TABLE OF CONTENTS

Author's Note		1
Introduction		2
1.	Escape Risk	5
2.	After the Fall	11
3.	Intuition	17
4.	The Path to Personal Reform	23
5.	Seven Simple Steps to Success	29
6.	The Cauldron of Adversity	54
7.	Meditation	67
8.	The Root of All Evil	77
9.	Preparing for Parole	82
10.	Insight	105
11.	Where the Woods Won't End	113
12.	Out of the Dark	119
13.	Evolution	130
14.	The Law Of Attraction	139
15.	The Golden Pony	147
16.	American Prisoner	152
Other Books by D. Razor Babb		154

AUTHOR'S NOTE

As a longtime resident and participant in the American prison experience one cannot help but begin to see and realize that it's the people you encounter that make the biggest impression and have the most significant impact on your own existence – for better or worse. The individuals operating on a higher plane, seemingly and actually utilizing a higher nature, lifting you up by their mere presence; and the loud, obnoxious, cruel, bitter, brutal, violent, loathsome characters – pulling you down in equal proportion, bringing out our own base nature … one begins to tire of the struggle between good and evil, without and within, and ultimately chooses a path (consciously or otherwise).

It is the purpose of <u>American Prisoner</u> (the book and perhaps series of books) to provide prisoners with an easy to read, easy to follow, self-help guide by which they are inspired to become aware of, develop and use their higher nature to become a better, more fully developed person.

<u>American Prisoner</u> takes the seven most basic, fundamental, easy to comprehend and implement philosophic strategies (gleaned from seven thousand years of writings and teachings) and presents them in a manner that allows the reader to absorb, understand and apply the condensed stratagems in a useful, present day light.

The book strives to offer the material in an interesting, reader friendly manner, without preaching or condemning. <u>American Prisoner</u> is inclusive, non-discriminatory or judgmental in source and intended audience. The author is a former news reporter and author of several novels and utilizes writing techniques from both realms, combined with a lifetime of exhaustive research and application of self-help, philosophic and spiritual investigation and research to present a comprehensive, informative, digestible and enjoyable go-to, self-help manual for the modern American Prisoner.

We present the enclosed material with sincere gratitude and appreciation for your perusal.

INTRODUCTION

I had lost everything – wife, children, career, hopes, dreams, aspirations, freedom …. I thought I couldn't sink any lower, but I was wrong. A sixty foot fall during a failed escape attempt left me a paraplegic, and destroyed a self-image based on physicality, leaving me basically defenseless in an environment where might was right and being able to fight and stand your ground is imperative to survival. If I was going to continue on I'd have to develop a completely different mindset where intellect and spirit took precedence over brawn, bravado, appearance and a concept of masculinity that was etched into my consciousness and belief system as deeply and inexorably as a prison tattoo. It would require operating from a totally foreign paradigm from that which I'd lived my entire life.

How had it come to this? How had I allowed myself to fall to these depths? And, what could I do to not only gain understanding as to what led me to such a desperate situation, but also rise from the ashes and begin again? Could it even be done?

I'd always found self-help and psychology texts to be insightful and of help for inspiration and guidance. But somehow the teachings hadn't been enough to forestall disaster. I needed more. Over the next seventeen years I read, studied and absorbed everything I could get my hands on in the fields of self-help, psychology, spirituality, sociology, philosophy, mysticism, the occult and anything to do with behavioral cause and effect and finding inner peace. I delved deep into the inner workings of mind and soul to try and uncover the complex mysteries of higher awareness and interconnectedness.

Along the way I've found some solid truths and eye-opening revelations that reveal that not only can a renewed life be achieved for myself, but it is available to any and all who diligently and honestly seek freedom and enlightenment. I discovered that all I had lost was, in fact, a minor price to pay for all that I gained.

I also found that with a higher understanding comes a higher purpose – mine is to cut through the clutter of the endless volumes of self-help, spirituality and philosophy and present a comprehensive, no nonsense, easy to follow personal self-help and rehabilitation guide for every man or woman who has found himself adrift in a sea of uncertainty and confusion and is trying to right his ship and set a course to safe harbor and discover a peaceful, purposeful existence no matter where he is.

It is my sincere hope and belief that others may benefit from my mistakes, toil and discoveries, and find their own higher nature and peaceful existence above and beyond the cage of what we so often settle for, never knowing the wondrous possibilities available to and within us all.

American Prisoner

D. Razor Babb

CHAPTER ONE: ESCAPE RISK

As I crouched atop the one-man rec cage and reached up to cut the last strands of wire fencing that separated inside from out, I was thinking: "If they're gonna catch me, now would be a good time."

It had taken six months of intense labor, calculated planning, opportune timing and good luck to get to this point. I had cash money, street clothes, a place to go, sixty feet of sheet rope, and an unwavering belief in my ability to pull this seemingly impossible stunt off. No one has ever escaped from L.A. County Jail's Highpower, it's the highest security section of the jail. That's where they keep the most violent, notorious and high-risk inmates. Gang shot callers, guys down from death row, multiple murderers, and escape risks. I was the latter, having been found in possession of a hacksaw blade at court early in my confinement. That had been my first clumsy attempt, this one was the culmination of over five years of scheming.

I was in the county jail for nearly six years, the five I did in Highpower was the best time I've ever done. You wouldn't think anyone would say that, after being locked in a tiny cell 24-7, strip-searched, shackled and cuffed behind the back any time you come out. Handcuffed to the table during attorney visits, behind glass for regular visits, one-and-a-half hours of rec time in a cage on the roof once a week – and, liable to get stabbed, cut or killed on the way to the shower. When you're surrounded by killers, you gotta watch your step, and your mouth. A wrong move either way could be your last.

In spite of all that, and regardless of reputation, the guys you encounter in Highpower are some of the most intelligent, honorable and respectful individuals you could ever meet. It's all about respect on those rows – you have to give it to get it, you gotta earn it to survive.

When I was there, 1994 to 1999, rows A, B, and C were the regulars. Twenty-five one-man cells per row, side-by-side. D row was new arrivals, orientation while being sorted out; E, F, and G were protective custody. O.J. was there at the time, he had all of G row to himself and was treated extremely well, a whole lot better than the rest of us. Celebrities get handled with kid gloves, with the media lime-light on them, high-priced lawyers and star-struck guards. But, when it comes down to it, they're locked in that cell just like everybody else.

The Menendez brothers, Joe Hunt (Billionaire Boy's Club), Chuck Rathbun (Raiderette killer), a string of rappers, movie guys and high-profilers, they all passed through during my time there. I was neighbors with Joe Hunt for a while. I'd have to say that he is probably the most intelligent person I've ever known, despite the two or three murders that are attributed to him. He found meditation and soul-awareness, post-murders, and shared that universal interconnectedness with me ... along with a vast knowledge of legal expertise. He's the best attorney I've personally known, and a master debater.

Joe's mentoring gave me a working knowledge of law beyond what a law school could provide. And four to five hours of meditation a day opened my mind and spirit to vast possibilities and limitlessness. That belief in no limits led to my lying atop the rooftop fencing and peering over the side of the jail, dropping the rope the last sixty feet to freedom. Three guards sat less than thirty feet away, another four or five monitored video surveillance screens. There are only ten Highpower cages and we're separated by fencing from the hundred or so mainline inmates who were roaming around the other half of the rec area ... most of them staring at me.

With adrenaline pounding in my ears, I knew there would be no going back. For the first time in over five years I was feeling the air of freedom on my face – it was exhilarating, and fleeting. It took six months to inconspicuously saw through the thick gauge wire of the cage, a little at a time. I had to get into the same cage every time, camouflage the cut marks and ultimately smuggle street clothes, cash, a hacksaw blade and sixty feet of rope to the roof ... after a strip search, handcuffed and escorted. Not easy, but not impossible.

The rooftop rec yard is situated four stories (each story about fifteen feet high) above the front corner of the jail. That section is beyond the areas that are fenced in with razor wire (on the ground). The concrete wall that comprises the back section of the Highpower cages drops into an alcove atop the administration offices. By our late afternoon rec time the offices are mostly empty. The front of that area of the jail is the visitor's entrance where a variety of civilians and jail personnel mill about. A few times to rec and I realized that directly on the other side of that back wall of the cage you could drop into that alcove unseen, jump the remaining few feet from the administrative offices and stroll out front and blend in with the crowd like anybody else. But first, you had to get out of the cage, cut through the fencing that covered the roof, and manage the drop.

Securing the tools, manufacturing the rope, obtaining the other articles took time. Hiding the stuff was even more difficult. It was supposed to be three of us going. One guy caught the chain to state prison, the other beat four of five murders and decided to try and win the fifth. I was going solo and got the green light from the shot callers for E-day. Getting that load of gear to the roof was a heady experience in itself. The guard is two feet in front of you, watching every move during a strip search – it's sleight of hand magic with a lot more than applause at stake. After I'd stripped and been searched, I simply reached over and picked up a different pair of pants, already packed with the gear. My heart was in my throat as he locked the cuffs behind my back, I just hoped he didn't notice the bulge from the bulky rope and that the weight of it didn't pull my pants down.

We're escorted four at a time to the roof, by three guards. Once I was in the cage I immediately cut the last remaining bits of heavy wire. I'm through. Every muscle is taut, I can see everything, I can hear everything, but I'm blocking out all distractions, fear or doubt. The general population inmates are giving me a pretty good eye, I'm signaling them to keep walking, mind their own business, and for God's sake, quit staring! Months, years really, of meticulous planning were culminating in these final minutes. I looked around, bent the wires back, grabbed the rope and hit the hole. Snag #1, it's too small! I'd miscalculated by inches. I'd have to cut three more thick wires, and time's running out. Only about thirty minutes of rec time is left.

The previous six months I'd slowly and deliberately done the cutting. Now I'm balls to the wall, full-tilt sawing on those bars like a wolf gnawing off its own leg to get free from a trap. The cage is shaking and rattling, the muscles in my arms are screaming and I'm sweating a puddle. I'm using a Vaseline-type ointment on the three inch blade to reduce friction and the blade is red hot from the frantic sawing. Noise from huge air-conditioner units on top of the roof are covering the commotion, I hope.

In a few minutes I'm through and don't hesitate to bend the bars back. I sling the rope over my shoulder and crawl out of the cage. There's no time for doubt or nerves, I shimmy up the side of the cage and crouch on top. I'm going. The cross meshing of the cage wiring creates an optical illusion from the guard's station. It appears you can see into the cages as you look down the row of ten, but the meshing distorts clear vision. In cage four the illusion is just right. I'm only thirty feet or so away from them, but I'm invisible. Two minutes more and I'm through the regular gauge fencing that covers the roof. I slip through and lay prone, looking over the side. It's eerily bizarre and surreal.

I know I could get shot doing this, or jumped by a pack of enraged guards and Rodney King'd into oblivion. But, my motivation and belief in my plan and ability far outweigh any lingering doubts. I'd just won a jury trial on a twenty-five-to-life case, representing myself. The odds of a prisoner acting as his own attorney, presenting a case to a jury and winning is off the charts. Using the same mindset and principles, clearly, fear was not part of the equation. In fact, over-confidence could be my only failing.

I'm lying on the rooftop fencing outside the confines of the jail, cages, guards, with nothing but open sky above and a sixty foot drop below. I secure the rope on a previously located drain pipe, drop it over the side and slide over the edge. The last minute frenzy of sawing had left ointment on my hands and my muscles are badly fatigued. Almost immediately I began slipping on the rope ... then sliding uncontrollably. The rope is burning through my fingers ... it's too thin, I should have made gloves, I needed more knots, whatever the problem(s) it's too late for solutions. I've escaped, but now I'm falling to my death.

When I come to I'm staring up at the sky. I attempt to crawl away but can't move. My freedom lasted only a few moments

I've read, and found through experience, that it's not what occurs in a life that defines us – but how we react to it … what we make of it. Every calamity has within it a lesson we may learn. The significance of suffering is important in human development, as it forces us to face the darkness – within ourselves, within others … and compels us to turn towards the light of our true, higher nature.

Finding the lesson in times of extreme adversity can be the most difficult thing imaginable. The lessons I needed to learn still lay before me.

CHAPTER TWO: AFTER THE FALL

After the fall I had to face some pretty significant changes. Coming from a no limits, anything was possible mindset to lying motionless in a hospital bed while they performed repeated surgeries on me just to save my life was a real roller coaster. The operations alone were enough to shake me to my soul. Waking up in the middle of surgery, abdomen cut wide open and organs laid out in grisly display as they worked on my spine was ghastly ... horrifying. Why were they even trying to save me? My life was over, I was going to waste away in a cell someplace, anyway, what was the purpose? I used every bit of meditational knowledge and experience I had to go as deep as I could and will myself to die. Just let me die.

Cruel irony. I'd done everything I could to escape those bonds that held me, and had come within a hair's breadth of success. Now, similarly and conversely, I was pushing the envelope to escape once again ... this time, a concentrated effort towards true finality. But, for whatever reason, this too would be denied.

Over the next months I lay in a jail hospital bed, trying to heal, reading everything I could get my hands on for distraction, meditating, exercising as I could. Willing myself to die. I'd spent a lifetime, forty-two years, relying on my physicality and sexual magnetism to define my self-worth. All that had been shattered and lost in an instant. I would have to switch from a self-perception and image based on my physical self to much more intellectual – spiritual paradigm and rebuild from scratch even while dealing with the physical limitations and unrelenting pain.

They had me on a pretty heavy dosage of morphine. I'd have to kick that first. If I was going to aspire to a more mentally acute and spiritually aware existence, I wasn't going to accomplish that by being a dope fiend. I needed a clear head. Weening from morphine was excruciating. To this day the pain is nearly intolerable. But kicking pain-killers is something I never want to face again. No wonder so many people get hooked. One shot and everything is okay again. You don't feel anything – physically or mentally. The easy way out. Except there's nothing easy about drug dependency. I feel fortunate that it's not something I'm attracted to, I have enough problems.

How had it come to this? How had I gotten to where I was, how does anyone? More than two and a half million prisoners in America. We confine a larger percentage of our populace than any other country. An odd statistic for a nation built on 'freedom'. Don't get me wrong, I don't blame anyone for my own troubles. I've found the culprit who caused all my misfortune, and he knows who he is. All I need to get a glimpse of the perpetrator is a mirror. But what about all the rest of these guys? Do they need to be here?

More than 95 percent of prisoners are eventually released, roughly 600,000 heading back to the streets, and more than that coming back inside every year. Since the war on crime, get tough on crime mantra began its self-perpetuating wave in the 1980's, the main concern of crime policy has been to get criminals off the streets. Very little consideration or forethought has gone into developing a long-term strategy for coping not only with the offenders, but the impact on society. Nearly two-thirds of released prisoners will be back, charged with new crimes. Forty percent come back within three years. Something is very wrong in that.

Based on Department of Justice statistics, inmate population began its meteoric rise between 1984 and 1994, climbing to approximately 500 people confined per 100,000 population. By the year 2000, along with the 2.5 million incarcerated, 4.9 million individuals were under some form of supervision, parole or probation … over 7 million under the control of criminal justice overseers. Big Brother on steroids. And if we have learned anything, things tend to get worse before they get better.

With the size of the ex-offender community rising to six times that of the current inmate population, this demographic needs to be recognized as a relevant factor in the discussion of a broad range of subjects …not the least being: public safety. If you lock a dog in a cage and mistreat it, poke at it, kick it, let it live with other more violent and predator dogs, how can you possibly be surprised when somebody gets bitten when the door is finally opened and the dog is let out?

In the 1970's and 80's when rehabilitation and reform were replaced with the iron fist of containment and retribution, the die was cast toward what we are experiencing today. Brute force management produces a harder criminal. The average length of sentences imposed and served increased by nearly 40 percent between 1985 and 1999. Crime did not become more serious, but punishment did. The number of drug offenders processed into the system increased more than ten-fold during this time, from 16 percent of inmates to more than 60 percent. Making the war on drugs one of the most consequential developments of our generation, contributing generously to the prison boom and focusing largely on the poorest, most desperate of our populace.

Drug offenders are the single largest category of admissions to state and federal prisons. The chance of being incarcerated for a drug offense increased between the years 1980 – 1992 by 500 percent, and the average sentence term doubled. The move toward mass incarceration isn't directed solely at drug abusers or violent offenders; small-time drug dealers, addicts, the homeless, and the mentally ill are all being warehoused in penitentiaries. Where the pen was once a last resort for the worst criminals, it is now the main 'solution' for dealing with (largely) urban social undesirables.

As homeless shelters and mental health treatment centers steadily lost funding over the past decades, prison construction has increased eleven fold, twice the rate of education, healthcare, and public welfare spending combined. With a more than $60 billion annual budget – prisons have become the single largest provider of housing, meals and healthcare for the poor and indigent.

Rehabilitation and even mild concern for societal reintegration aren't even a part of prison administration conversation. Find 'em a bed, put 'em on meds – if they act up, lock 'em down.

Personally, I've never been diagnosed with any type of mental disorder and I take no medications or drugs. Yet, in the pod of fourteen I'm housed in, nine of these guys are on some type of psych meds, some nearly incoherent. The others are either physically handicapped or faking some handicap. The message is clear – the prison administration views the physically and mentally handicapped as one in the same, at least in terms of housing. Based on personal observation and living in close quarters with these people, I believe most of them should never have been locked up in the first place, and given even moderate guidance or opportunity, would be better off in some form of substance abuse treatment facility – someplace where they might obtain self-help training or counselling and guidance.

After 23 years inside, disciplinary free, with no further escape attempts and the days of hanging with tough guys behind me, I've landed in a purgatory of old folks, wheelchairs, psych patients, and worst of all … short termers. From the land of J-cats and idiots I look back in fond remembrance to the days in Highpower and similar places. Even though if I'd have been able to stay in that environment my life span most likely would have been greatly shortened. You have to 'put work in' in those places, the kind of work that ends up catching up with you.

The powers that be determined that in my depleted physical condition I was no threat and 'compatible' with guys in places like this. I fought it, to no avail … finally accepting a deal for single man cell that lasted another nine years. They say we all eventually get what we deserve, but nobody deserves this – the dreaded level two dorm. Two hundred fifty of the most disgusting, disrespectful, loud, obnoxious, ill-mannered, ignorant, and socially maladjusted individuals you could ever throw together.

What a wonderful opportunity to implement all the philosophy, self-help, spiritual enlightenment and higher learning I've been studying and working on for all these years. It's a far cry from where I've been and what I've seen and experienced in Highpower and other places … and a whole new and different set of challenges. As humans, and primates, we somehow adapt to our environment, though. And if not for adversity we would become complacent and stagnant. Therefore, I welcome the challenges I'm faced with and appreciate the universe's gift that affords me an opportunity for further growth.

When I was single-celled all those years, I took up writing. I founded and published a newsletter that eventually went national (*The Corcoran Sun*), wrote and published several novels and won a couple of national writing competitions. I even helped other writers complete and publish their own work. I'm currently publishing a writers' workshop book to teach prisoners how to write and publish from the inside. It's difficult to continue the writing in an environment like this. There are always guys milling around, noise all the time, no privacy or solitude. It can be quite maddening.

But, on the flip side, you never know how things will work out and even in the most seemingly dire circumstances sometimes fate, luck, destiny or synchronicity intervene to surprise us. In a lot of the philosophy, self-help, and higher awareness texts I've read they insist there are no coincidences, they're very adamant on that point. We all get our very own special set of circumstances and everything and everyone that's placed in our path arrives there for a reason. I guess that explains why I met Keith Kakugawa.

CHAPTER THREE: INTUITION

"Intuition: A sudden immersion of the soul into the universal current of life, where the histories of all people are connected, and we are able to know everything, because it is all written there."

from: <u>The Alchemist</u>, by Paulo Coelho

I've been in the prison system for a while now, since 1993 this term, and along the way have fortunately stumbled onto some very interesting writings, situations, and people. In Paolo Coelho's mega-bestselling novel, <u>The Alchemist</u>, a shepherd boy named Santiago travels from his homeland in Spain to the Egyptian desert in search of treasure buried in the Pyramids. What starts out as a journey to find worldly riches turns into a discovery of the treasure found within. The author sublimely states within the text, "To realize one's destiny is a person's only obligation."

Coelho's family had him institutionalized three times for trying to pursue his destiny of writing. He finally immigrated to America from Brazil and realized his dream ... writing <u>The Alchemist</u> in two weeks. It's sold over 52 million copies in 117 countries and has been translated into 41 languages.

I've known of the book for some time, but never read it. During the writing of this transcript, I happened upon it, seemingly by coincidence. I immediately swept it up and began reading. It's mesmerizing. I was taken aback by how similar it seemed to be to my own first novel, <u>Icicle Bill</u> –an action, adventure tale of a man on a journey who encounters many strange characters and learns different things from each one. He ultimately learns that if we persevere onward, even in the face of adversity, and take each step with noble intent, we will succeed in realizing our destiny.

Another key point of the narrative of both books is that people appear in our lives at just the right time to assist us in our endeavors. As if the "universe conspires to help us accomplish our goals and fulfill our desires."

After completing several fiction novels, I decided I would try my hand at writing a sort of self-help, personal rehabilitation bit. I've read so many self-help, philosophy, higher-awareness works that I thought I might be able to combine the vast library and wide-spectrum of teachings into a more digestible and condensed version. And, make it more interesting to read for the average person who wouldn't normally be drawn to the matter of personal rehabilitation. It's similar to how I wrote <u>Icicle Bill</u>, which was a morality play with strong autobiographical content disguised as an action-adventure.

I had been approached by a small publisher to do an autobiography after the first story came out, and spent nearly a year completing it. It was so personal and revealing though, I decided to shelve it. Now, four or five fiction novels later, I began <u>American Prisoner,</u> and the only way I can really deliver it is through my own personal experience … with the integration of some of the stories of others I've met along the way. Just as Paulo Coelho's shepherd, Santiago, meets strangers along the way that help in his quest, so have I. And, similarly, all have contributed to making my own journey richer and more fulfilling.

When I got transferred from cell-living to a dorm I thought my writing days were most likely over. The noise, distractions, noise. But I kept at it as well as I could and one day Keith Kakugawa approached me and asked if I wanted to read something. It was his own autobiography, <u>A Tale of Two</u>

Brothers, by David Burgess. Keith, it turns out, is a boyhood friend of another brother from Hawaii, Barack Obama, and played a key role in Obama's search for his identity and quest for personal self-hood.

Keith knew about my writing and proposed a project – a treatise on the prison industrial complex and the malfeasance and inequities foisted on the American public selling incarceration as the cure-all prescription for crime management. To me, it seemed like it was meant to be. All my struggles and life and writing experience – Keith's contacts, education and ability to get things done. There are far too many guys locked up for way too long and the public is, for the most part, completely ignorant of the real tragedies that are occurring right under their noses in the name of law and order. It's time to not only raise the curtain on the drama, but give individuals who are in need the tools necessary to cope and transcend the incapacitating yoke of repression and incarceration.

To me, it seemed odd that a boyhood friend of Obama's, who had attended an elite high school in Hawaii, Punahou, established as a prep school for missionaries and businessmen's children in 1841 who wanted a Boston education for them without having to ship them stateside, would end up in the same dorm as the likes of me and other convicts. Punahou is a 'feeder' school to the Ivy League colleges, their academic reputation is stellar. Their alumni list reads like an all-star Who's Who.

Google lists literally eighteen pages of Punahou School notable alumni, including, Olympic athletes, world champions, pro athletes, top medical doctors, educators, researchers, civil rights leaders, elected representatives, military leaders and heroes, entertainers, business leaders and philanthropists, authors, editors and journalists – including American On-Line founder Steven Case, the first woman Navy Admiral, Alma Lau Grocki, eBay founder Pierre Omidyar, golfer Michelle Wei, and football players Mosi Tatupu, Mark Tuninei and Manti Te'o – to name just a few.

In his teens, Barack Obama (known as Barry at the time) was being raised by his white grandparents. His mother was off in Indonesia, pursuing her own career, and his father was long gone and he never really knew Barack Senior. For a kid searching for his identity with the only Black influence in his life being television, he was naturally drawn to the two year older Keith, himself of mixed race and one of only a handful of Punahou's Black population. In Obama's autobiography, 'Dreams of My Father', he wrote:

"Despite the difference in age, we'd fallen into an easy friendship, due in no small part to the fact that together we made up almost half of Punahou's Black high school population. I enjoyed his company, he had a warmth and brash humor …."

Keith was referred to as 'Ray' in the book. They're still friends, even though the powers in the Democratic Party are sensitive to keeping real distance between the leader of the free world and a convicted felon, in fact and perception. More than once I brought up the topic of, why hasn't Obama done more for prison reform, considering the vast numbers of African-Americans incarcerated, it would only seem natural he'd be sensitive to the issue. Not only that, leading members of the Black community surely are insisting on the desperate need for accountability, or at the very least, some honest evaluation of the injustices and inequities. Even when the entire nation was focused on the race issue with the recent publicity of young Blacks being shot by police; to me, it appeared that Obama wasn't front and center as might have been expected – on scene, leading the country in an honest discussion of the underlying factors. Keith says, "They're not gonna let him." It's a chilling thought to consider, if the president can't do anything for prison reform, or isn't willing, who can?

For me, I feel I'm on a schedule, and a tight one. Obama's out in 2017, if the Republicans get back in, any inkling of a chance to bring up the topic on a national level is out the window. And if Hillary gets in, she's going to have her own problems just treading water. No excuses, though, we've gotta try.

So, you've got to wonder how a guy who went to the same elite school as the president, buddies with the man, went on to pursue a college degree and work in the financial field successfully for E.F. Hutton and others, winds up in a prison dorm in Central California with the likes of the rest of us. Drugs, mostly. A series of drug arrests during the time of the initiation of three-strikes. Once you're in the system it's like a black cloud that follows you around. For the tiniest infraction, or even suspicion of a technical violation, you're back inside. But, wherever any of us end up, we still have to own up and accept responsibility and carry our own water. Keith's doing that.

After spending twenty plus years studying the interconnectedness of the universe and all things therein and beyond, I tend to find a more meaningful reason for his being here at this time. Synchronicity. It was meant to be. My background as a news reporter, having been in the system for all this time, honing my writing skills to prepare me for something greater and more beneficial than simply reaching *The New York Time's* bestseller list or lining my own pockets. Maybe it was all designed for a greater purpose, finally presenting those inside and out with comprehensive, meaningful documentation of and a plan to help fix something that's beyond broken – it's, when simply stated, a real mess.

But, with an indefatigable determination, maybe some positive steps can be taken. I refuse to believe I've gone through all this for nothing, and that a childhood buddy of the President of the United States and I crossed paths in a place such as this, for no better reason than to comment on the crisis and needs of our fellow sufferers, without giving it a go.

Since everything I've read, studied, and absorbed teaches that there are no coincidences, there are lessons in every adversity, and intuition is a sudden immersion of the soul into the universal current of life ... I have to search for the meaning, follow my intuition, and strive to uplift myself and my community ... regardless of what community that is. Some observers might say, this particular community is the one most in need of uplifting.

Maybe it's not such a coincidence, after all, Keith and I find ourselves here.

CHAPTER FOUR: THE PATH TO PERSONAL REFORM

Let's be real about a crucial point – nobody's going to rehabilitate, reform, or redeem your life except you. You've got to want to change and improve or else all the excellent wonderment that's the world on the other side of felonious sin will remain a fairy tale and forever out of reach. That said, maybe you're ready for a little sociological makeover, we can all stand improvement. Look where our tough-guy, ego-dominated, self-loathing, look out for number one attitudes have gotten us so far. Or, as I like to say: it wasn't easy getting to where I am today, it took dedication and concentrated effort.

A very popular saying goes, "If you find yourself in a hole, stop digging."

That's the first thing we've got to do, stop digging. The same behavior that landed us inside is the sort of attitude that keeps us from being happy, pursuing loftier goals and finding our bliss. We've become complacent in our expectations and look outside of ourselves for comfort and joy. Things like sex, money, drugs, power, car, bitches & ho's, an strikin' a pose. Fool, you're chasin' smoke. All that fake glimmer and glam can't buy you outta this jam. Get real. You've got to go deeper than all that. I have to believe you may already know that, though.

There's a well-known author named Napoleon Hill who spent 25 years of his life studying and interviewing the greatest men of his time in order to come up with a step-by-step method that ordinary people could follow in order to achieve success. He wrote <u>Think and Grow Rich</u> and subsequent works and is considered one of the mainstays of the self-help field. His methodology involves persistence, well defined goals, positive thinking and noble intent. He insightfully writes that, "Anything the mind of man can conceive and believe, he can achieve." He finds that, ultimately, there is one single key that is capable of unlocking the mysteries of the universe, and that each of us has this ability within us, if we would just exercise it. That ability is: The power to control our own mind.

It sounds so simple, yet this one feat is so often beyond our grasp. Why is that? If we're not in control of our own mind, then who is?

I've got to tell you honestly, I've been studying this stuff for the better part of my lifetime and I still struggle with it. I've seen great people, smart, successful people who similarly struggle, so don't feel alone if you also find yourself feeling like the world is crashing down around you at times and there seems like no way out. We're human, nobody is perfect. But we have to begin to understand the principles that will bring us out of the dark and into the light. We all want to be happy, content, satisfied, at peace. The power to do that is within our grasp.

One very basic concept to understand in order to begin to gain control is this: All time is 'now'. Meaning, the future is yet to be, the past is gone. To live in either is useless, and, quite frankly, not possible. You can never change the past. The best you can do is to accept it, realize your mistakes and use the present moment to improve how your future moments will turn out. So since you only have this current moment to deal with, what if you decided to make it work for you? To decide that this moment: I feel good. I feel wonderful! I feel creative, kind, loving, beautiful, expansive, abundant, and receptive. It's your choice how you decide you want to feel this very moment.

Of course, you can also choose to feel grumpy, dour, sad, depressed, ugly, hateful, vengeful, jealous, scared, mean or evil. And when we're feeling any of those ways, how do you think things are going to go? You've only got this moment to live, it's your choice how you're going to feel, your choice how you're going to live. Make a choice.

Does all this sound difficult to you? Trying to improve yourself isn't the easiest task you'll ever undertake, but what good in life comes easily? Trying the easy route is what got most of us here in the first place. Now, we're trying to get out and get on with life and be able to find some form of contentment. Marcus Aurelius says of happiness: "It is all within yourself, in your way of thinking." Alfred Lord Tennyson defines it as: "The mastery of passions." Mark Twain's take on happiness: "Good friends, good books and a sleepy conscience." Of course, Twain also said, "When people ask me what I did with all the book money, I tell them I spent it all on whiskey and women ... the rest, I wasted." So you see, a sense of humor doesn't hurt, as well.

Most of us don't willingly take on difficult tasks. We have an innate tendency for the path of least resistance. In a recent *Entrepreneur Magazine* article, Nobel Prize-winning writer Daniel Kahneman was quoted as saying, "Our brains are primed to opt for the easier, quicker or more impulsive route." Making changes in our persona and outlook is a difficult task, and requires us to face formidable obstacles squarely, requiring a healthy dose of willpower.

Willpower is an assertion of self-control, the ability to manage thoughts, emotions, bad habits, and override momentary desires in order to reap long-term benefits. Willpower is something we can build up, like muscle mass. It is strengthened by self-regulation, controlling impulses, holding off indulgent behavior, and persevering for reward to come that might not be seen in the short-term.

Instant gratification seems so much sexier. I want it, I need it, I gotta have it ... now! Typical criminal mentality, but we're going for something greater here. You're going to build up your mental powers and begin to take control of your life. And there's nothing sexier than that! Believe it. You've got more than enough of what it takes inside of you to meet ANY challenge – you simply have to believe you do. That's the choice, it's all about mindset.

Every time you resist temptation it becomes easier to resist in the future. By using willpower, you build it. Regulating impulse control means choosing positive thoughts and behavior over negatives. Like choosing healthy food over junk, or a nice girl instead of a hoochie. Nothing wrong with a little sugar once in a while, but in the long run the clean stuff provides a better life and helps you sleep peacefully at night.

Researchers have found that rehearsing reactions to temptation or setbacks can help us resist negatives and overcome anxiety. Instead of reacting with the usual panic and stress when things go bad, you can teach the brain to have a different reaction. You create an "if-then" statement that triggers behavior you want to have in the future. For instance ... when you feel yourself ready to flare up over something, instead of automatically lighting that fuse, you can have the phrase ready:

"I'm in control of my own thoughts, I choose to be cool."

There's nothing cooler than a guy who refuses to get upset and can keep his head in tough situations. Remember, who is in control of YOU? When we ignite in hot-headed flames of rage or panic or confusion, it's actually a fear response. We've come to the end of our rational, intellectual reasoning and are lost in the abyss of frenzied mayhem. We go off because we don't know what else to do. But we can LEARN what to do and learn to control ourselves.

The reduction or control of fear is important in building willpower, it lowers stress levels and cuts the chances of making poor decisions based on irrational emotions. Positive emotions such as compassion, gratitude and love been show to expand focus and decrease fear. University of North Carolina's Barbara Fredrickson is one of the leading researchers on positive emotions and author of <u>Positivity</u>. She points out that positive emotions can undo the consequences of stress that undercut confidence and lead to negative thoughts and behavior.

You can choose to switch to positivity in an instant by taking the moment to think about something you are grateful for, or think of a particularly pleasant time or episode or event in your life. The instant you feel the heat rising you switch to that positive, pleasant thought and let it wash over and through you. In a positive, optimistic state, your brain is open to new ideas and solutions, not constricted by fear.

Think about it, what are you most grateful for? Try lingering on that for a few moments each day. Make a list of things you're grateful for and use it as a go-to mechanism every time you're feeling down, blue or angry.

Now, think of the most pleasant or memorable times of your life, visualize these experiences. Do you remember how you felt at the time they were happening? These are your go-to visualizations you will call up any time you begin to feel down and out or ready to snap. YOU are in control of how you think and what you think and how you feel. Take charge of yourself, take control.

Try this exercise: Each night when you lay down to sleep, think of three things that went well during the day, ask yourself why they went that way. You'll start recognizing positive events that previously went unnoticed and negativity is pushed aside in favor of good thoughts.

Start connecting with positive, energetic, happy people. Let the losers go. You'll begin to recognize that you have more good going on inside of you than you may have realized. There's a whole better world out there, and you'll begin noticing it once you take control of your own thoughts. I know you can do it, you have to believe it too.

CHAPTER FIVE: SEVEN SIMPLE STEPS TO SUCCESS

"To find peace, turn inside and look into your own heart. One who radiates love, attracts love and has love."

— DRB

Truth and revelation come not from any person, but from the source of all thought and thing. Conditions and circumstances we find ourselves in are not random, our lives are manifestations of our own design brought about consciously or otherwise. We create our life and destiny by our rejection of, or adherence to the higher source. Simply put, the thoughts that dominate one's mind dictate the quality and direction of existence. When we're out of sync with this higher energy it's like trying to swim upstream against the current of a powerful river. Everything is difficult, life is a struggle.

When we're in tune with the higher source, the river of life flows effortlessly, things, people, and circumstances are drawn to us to aid in our journey, and life is good. At any moment you can alter your own course, simply by gaining control of your own thoughts and feelings by focusing your attention on ideas and emotions that are in harmony with the source, finally rejoining the vast limitless ocean of thought from which everything and everyone began.

These are high concept theorems ultimately reached through centuries of study, research, and introspection and insight gained, in the present sense, via much investigation, analysis and toil. Herein, we break the higher teachings down, into an easy to follow seven step process which anyone may adopt and implement in order to live a better life.

SEVEN SIMPLE STEPS TO SUCCESS
– H<u>A</u><u>S</u> L<u>O</u><u>V</u>E –

In order to easily remember the seven steps we will employ the use of a simple mnemonic device, the acronym – HAS LOVE.

<u>H</u>ONESTY — to yourself and to others.

<u>A</u>SK FORGIVENESS — from those you have hurt and offer it to those who have hurt you.

<u>S</u>OUL AWARENESS — stop and listen to the voice inside, that's your soul, that which is interconnected to everyone else.

<u>L</u>IVE UNDER CONTROL — of your own mind; create your life by replacing negatives with positives.

<u>O</u>WN YOUR LIFE — by giving it away. Do something of benefit to and for others.

<u>V</u>OICE OF KINDNESS — speak kindly; be kind; treat others as you would like to be treated.

<u>E</u>NDLESS LOVE — listen to your heart, it knows the way. Live from a place of love and there are no limits on what you can accomplish.

This is a bare bones breakdown by which we may be able to easily and quickly gain control of our own lives. By memorizing the HAS LOVE principles, we can refer back to them repeatedly, reminding ourselves of who we are and who we wish to be. In the following pages we will delve into and dissect each principle to gain familiarity and understanding of the deeper concepts behind each, and thereby reap the rewards of knowledge.

HONESTY

You may be familiar with this story, it has been told many times in varying incarnations; however told, the moral remains intact.

There was a very rich man who wanted to do something for his community. He knew of a local carpenter who was out of work and having a hard time providing for his family, so he called him in and explained that he was going out of town for six months and he wanted the carpenter to build a house for him, under the condition that it be completed by the time he returned. The carpenter was elated to have found work and the two agreed upon an expense budget for materials and a fair salary for the carpenter; he wrote out a check in advance.

The rich man headed out and the carpenter got to work. From the very start he had a scheme to trim costs and squeeze out some extra profit by cutting every corner he could. He used the cheapest, most inferior materials and hired inexperienced workers and pushed then to work as fast as they could so he could save the money on wages to keep for himself. He covered up shoddy workmanship and mistakes with paint and plaster and finished just in time.

When the rich man returned he announced that the job was complete and handed over the keys. The rich man smiled warmly and handed he keys back. "My friend," he announced proudly, "Congratulations, you and your family get to live in the very house you built yourself!" He had intended all along for the house to be a gift for the carpenter and his family.

Each one of us is building our lives, brick by brick, from every thought we ponder, every word we say, every act we perform. The quality of our character is the material with which we construct our existence. Our intentions and the contents of our consciousness determine the outcome. If we want good results, if we want a quality life built on a solid foundation, honesty is the bedrock for a future that will stand the test of time.

Lies and deceit create suspicion and animosity. The judicial system has a very succinct way to deal with lies. A witness's entire testimony may be stricken from the record, every statement they've made disavowed and their credibility ruined if they're found to have lied under oath. It's really very simple. After you have lied, deceived, mislead, conned … anything you do or say is suspect.

Have you ever considered that it's just easier to be honest? No more trying to hide the truth or trying to remember the complicated web of lies that grew from the first one. No more looks of skepticism or disbelief. The most difficult and telling factor in being honest is – are you honest with yourself? Ask yourself these questions:

- How did you get here?
- Who is most responsible for your current situation?

If your answer is any more than a single word, you're not being honest with yourself. And if you can't even tell yourself the truth, how can you expect anyone else to believe in you?

If you build your life on a foundation of lies it's like building a house on quicksand; it'll never stand for anything. If you think you have to lie and cheat and steal and deceive to get by in the cruel world, you're still just lying to yourself. You're going to have to get past this in order to build a solid life. No time better than the present to begin.

There's a reason HONESTY is the first step in H-A-S-L-O-V-E, it's the foundation on which everything else is built.

When you tell the truth, when you do the right thing, you can hold your head high and look anyone straight in the face and know that regardless of anything else, your word is good. And the best feeling there is, is being able to look in a mirror and know that's true.

FORGIVENESS

You have to forgive to be forgiven. You have to forgive before you can forget.

Forgiveness is one of the principles that appears over and over in all the self-help, philosophy texts and teachings. I can't emphasize how important this step is without telling you a story about my own experience.

At the age of four my divorced mother met and married a man whose presence dominated and impacted my young life in such a significant manner, that it would be unconscionable to write this chapter without mention. For the next nine years I lived under the tyranny and abuse of this monster.

By all outward appearances, this was a fine, upstanding citizen in the small Missouri community where we had migrated. Hard-working, personable, and to all – seemingly an honest, reliable, decent person. To all except my mother and me. The psychological and physical abuse began almost immediately, first with whippings for minor infractions – then, all out beatings and constant verbal tirades. The worst part was listening at night when he would beat my mother into submission and be unable to do anything to stop it.

At age thirteen I began rebelling – running away, acting out, beginning to show outward contempt. The shipped me off to whatever relative would take me and I couldn't have been happier to get out of there. I thought that at long last I was free from the yoke of pain and torment. I had no concept of the deep psychological trauma that had seeped into my subconscious, that nine years of torture had left scars on my psyche that I wouldn't become aware of until many years later while lying in a prison cell, wondering how I had allowed myself to get to where I was.

From the tender age of four, I had begun to learn and develop such a profound capacity for hatred that grew and developed over the next nine years, that by the time I was no longer in the situation that cultivated it, it was too deeply rooted to extract. Not without serious professional help or years of study, research and self-introspection. And what was possibly the worst part was, I had covered it so well with an outward appearance of congeniality and good manners, that I'd fooled myself into believing that I was 'all right'.

But, of course, the lengthy prison sentence evinces otherwise.

In times of grave stress or during periods of manic-depression, without any self-awareness or coping skills, what was hidden inside would appear unexpectedly and manifest into a rage borne from the hostile environment of enmity and malice that had nourished it for so long.

I had held that hatred in for so long that once it was released, it overrode every other personality trait. It was so strong, when in full rage mode, it was uncontrollable, particularly for a young man not fully developed emotionally or psychologically.

It took coming to prison, being locked away in that cell in county jail –

finding meditation (by luck, happenstance, coincidence, fate, synchronicity) and beginning to delve deep inside before I started to realize that all my problems, and all the hurt I'd caused other people, was due to the unresolved hatred I had inside for that sick, psycho, abusive son-of-a-bitch who beat and abused my mother and me for nine long years.

Through meeting Joe Hunt and being introduced to meditation, I discovered that I do have a soul inside, I am a soul inhabiting a body, and that all souls are interconnected. You can't hurt another without hurting yourself. And I had done so much hurt that it felt like I'd never be able to overcome it all.

But there's something wonderful about learning about the deeper forces that rule the universe and higher awareness. There's something going on out there that's so much bigger than the problems of puny individuals, and you can create your own experience here on earth through understanding.

You can even begin living your life anew from this very moment on and be forgiven your past. There's just one little catch – you have to forgive in order to be forgiven, in order to be free from the past. You can't hold on to the hatred and expect good things to come. You see, thoughts are things and the things you think about you're attracting into your life. We'll get into that deeper, later. But you have to trust me on this, I've done all the research, read all the books, experimented in my own life.

Until you honestly forgive those who have hurt you, that bitterness will keep showing up in your own life. You have to go deep inside and yank all that animosity out and throw it away. It's not helping you. And you can't just 'say' you forgive, but still harbor the ill-feelings. I've tried that, it doesn't work. You have to whole-heartedly FORGIVE!

How are you going to forgive the guy who killed your brother? Or the one who burned your house down? Or beat your mother into submission? Yeah, not easy. Nothing good usually is. But once you really do it, such a great weight will be lifted from your shoulders that you'll wonder why it took so long.

In order to live your own life, in order to be in control of your own destiny, you have to forgive. Otherwise, you're not the one in control. If you're holding onto that hate, guess who is? Once I realized that very point, it wasn't as difficult to let go. I know it's hard, I also know it can be done. You can do this, and until you realize it and put it into action, you're stuck where you are. And that ain't cool. Come to the light ... step out of that shadow and move into the light. You can't say no one has shown you the way. I'm showing you now. It's up to you to take that step.

SOUL AWARENESS

It seems odd, at times, how things work out. Just as I've come to the point in this manuscript where we discuss the seeking of soul (not in a religious sense, but in a broader more expansive context where everyone and everything melds into a confluence of energy) Keith Kakugama came to me and sought some words of solace for his departed Uncle Sam. Not a blood uncle, but in Hawaii any member of a close-knit community is considered family, 'ohana', they call it. I was reminded of how when my own father passed it felt as though on his way out he lingered; somehow from beyond he managed to pull a few strings and reunite my sister and me, who had been lost to one another for so long.

As in Uncle Sam's passing – he, who had been a source of inspiration as a patriarch of the ohana that included Keith and Barry and so many others growing up on the island – somehow seems to have a presence in this dreary dorm in a California prison when Keith speaks of him and tells us of who he was and how he impacted lives. And, even odder how only days ago at the beginning of this book Keith and I were complaining and bemoaning the fact that Obama hadn't lifted a finger for prison reform, et al ... and now, this past week, he commutes the sentences of 46, visiting El Reno prison in Oklahoma and focusing the national spotlight on criminal justice reform.

A massive 'coincidence' in a universe where there are no coincidences. Is it a stretch to consider that Uncle Sam had an ethereal hand in events? Keith and I at the same place with the same idea of writing a tome on prison reform – he with the contacts to get it out there, me with the ability to put the words together in a manner that might be palatable to the masses, the topic becoming a leading anthem for 18 of the current presidential contenders in the 2016 election – all of this occurring seemingly simultaneously.

I don't know that I have the ability to convey to the reader within the parameters of these pages the concept of interconnectedness. And not simply in reference to a 'physical sense' where science and quantum mechanics point to the fact that everything in our galaxy is made up of the same matter. Every star, our own sun, every planet, every molecule on earth, water, animal, vegetable, mineral made up of the same elements. Interconnectedness goes beyond that. Our very souls, the essence of our being is a part of the exact same energy that everything is derived from. To the point of being no longer matter, but 'thought'.

Taking that concept to the next step, consider this – every thought we project, especially those infused with emotion and feeling, is put out into the ether and attracts like thoughts and energy. So, when we think of loved ones departed with open hearts, wrought with emotional sentiment, it is not beyond the realm of belief that we might experience some reactive dynamic.

Those of a religious ilk refer to it as prayers being answered. Followers of the eastern rites speak of such things during deep meditative states. Whatever it is and whatever you call it, you have to admit there's a lot going on out there that man and society does not yet fully understand.

And you don't have to understand it to make it work for you in your own life. Most of us don't know how electricity works, and yet we make viable use of it every day.

When I was sixteen I was driving back from a concert in St. Louis. It was about three in the morning and the only other vehicles on the freeway were diesel trucks. I was passing a caravan of three tractor-trailers, they were in the middle lane and I was doing about 70 mph in the left lane. A concrete median on my left divided the freeway, the trucks were following one another closely. When I was even with the first truck I suddenly saw a huge patch of water that had accumulated in the lane just ahead of me. When I hit that water the van I was driving began to hydroplane and suddenly lurched to the right, toward the diesel. I immediately jerked the steering wheel to the left, and at the speed I was going, it caused the front of the van to crash into the median with such force that it propelled the back end into the middle lane, conveniently spinning in between the space between the first and second truck. The force and momentum was so great that the van kept spinning, and the front end then spun into the space between the second and third truck.

When I looked up the front of that third diesel truck was coming at me, inches away, heading directly at the front windshield of the van at 70 mph. There was no doubt in my mind that this was my last moment alive. I closed my eyes and turned that steering wheel as hard as I could, yelling out loud, "Oh God, this is it!" That's when things got weird.

Suddenly, I mean as fast as the blink of an eye, I found myself watching myself from the back of the van. I mean, I literally could see myself from outside of my body, I was watching this drama play out in real time, right before my own eyes – or whatever visual sense that was occurring. I can still see it, I can see the exact clothes I was wearing and it's as real as anything I've ever experienced.

Just as quickly as it happened, I was suddenly back in my body and the trucks were whizzing on down the highway, the van was scraping against the median, and I had survived a harrowing near-death experience. Now, I wasn't a religious person, by any stretch. The "Oh God!" exclamation was a reactionary utterance, and desperate plea, although not contemplated as such – evinced by the fact that I had but a split second to react. And, what's perhaps more interesting, I didn't understand that my soul had left my body. I was sixteen and monumentally ignorant of anything that didn't wear a short skirt, play a mean lead guitar lick, or couldn't be rolled and smoked. All I knew was, 'that was weird'.

It wasn't until several years later when I happened to be reading a book named Life After Life where true-life survivors of near-death experiences related their encounters, that I found out that was what happened to me. I bemoan the fact that even when I realized what had occurred, it didn't change anything (at that time). I continued on in my ignorance and wasn't the least bit inclined to try and understand the implications. I wasn't ready, it was way too immense for me to understand. But, live on and learn.

What I feel is one of the most important points of this event in my life is that fact that I'm not religiously affiliated, it's definitely not affixed to any of that influence. And because I was so young and dumb, I had no preconceived notion of 'soul awareness', so the event is untainted, it just 'happened'. It's only all these years later that I began to attach significance and have some semblance of understanding.

You see, because of this happening, I'm acutely aware that 'soul' is a real thing, literally. When higher awareness teachings talk of our souls inhabiting our bodies, and it is our soul that is the true essence of our being, I'm not just getting that on an intellectual, conceptual level – I know it to be true because I experienced it. Thus, when these learned teachers go on to explain that all souls are a part of the same energy and we're all interconnected, I can make the leap to believing quite easily, and believe it is important for you to begin to conceive and understand, as well.

If you can go inside yourself and find your soul, the things that brought you to where you are today will all start to make sense. The things that have troubled you your whole life will begin to melt away. You will be able to move toward a place where creativity, kindness, love, beauty, expansiveness, abundance, and receptivity reign.

If you want to rehabilitate yourself, you are going to have to recognize and find your own soul within. If you can do that, all the pieces of the puzzle that is your life will begin to fall into place.

LIVE UNDER CONTROL

Create the life you want to live by controlling your own mind; never let circumstances dictate what is and what will be.

In an enlightening article in a Buddhist publication, Paolo Mecacci cites the research of Professor Martin Seligman who conducted in-depth studies on "acquired impotence", the long-term effects of exposure to critical circumstances in which people feel at a dead-end, making them feel personally and socially impotent. The increasing sense of uselessness blocks the will to resolve difficult situations, leading to apathy, withdrawal, inactivity, and a belief that anything in their life is beyond their control This causes an abandonment of any sense of personal power and self-worth.

This dynamic is certainly nothing new. Man has been grappling with these inner demons since the dawn of humanity. In the classic Italian opera, "Pagliacci" (The Clown) by Leoncavallo (1858-1919) in Act One, "Vesti la Guibba" (Put on Your Costume), Pagliacci is sitting in front of the mirror, putting on his make-up before a performance, chiding himself to act!

"Vesti la Guibba"

> To act! While in the grip of wild frenzy;
> I no longer know what I am saying or doing.
> And yet I must – make yourself do it!
> Bah, you are not a man! Ah! Ah!
> You are the clown!
> Put on your costume and paint your face white
> The people pay to see you and want to laugh.
> And if Harlequin steals you Columbine,
> Laugh, clown, and everyone will applaud!
> Transform your trembling and tears to buffoonery,
> Your sobbing and despair into a grimace.
> Ah! Laugh, clown, for your shattered love!
>
> Laugh at the sorrow which is poisoning your heart!

Pagliacci's wife has been unfaithful. He is torn between his deep, undeniable love and his jealous rage and damaged ego that are crying out for revenge and justice. He's contemplating murder. And yet, even as he mourns the gilded love, he realizes the character he plays, the clown, is the part he plays in real life … and the audience doesn't know, or care, of his pain and torment – they just want to laugh, only seeing the painted face that covers his sorrow. Drowning in a sea of despair, Pagliacci feels all is lost, he can't decide what to do, he feels impotent.

This sense of loss of control is especially prevalent in situations where people have no employment, education or training – a phenomenon occurring at an alarming rate outside, especially in poorer communities where prospects appear sparse, and certainly correlative in prisoner's lives where hope is at a premium.

Many times the reason we do wrong acts is that we feel impotent, like nothing is within our control. We numb that feeling with drugs, pull a gun to feel empowered, engage in random, frequent sex acts to bolster our ego – short-term, momentary sedatives that mask the larger problems and in most instances make things worse.

Prolonged periods of an apathetic mindset creates a condition called "passive conformity", a term which describes the process whereby feelings of impotence and anxiety caused by uncertainty lead to an acceptance of an unfavorable situation … eventually causing a person to lower personal expectations in order to avoid disappointment, failure and frustration. Ultimately, hope is extinguished.

It is this debilitating mindset of impossibility which inhibits and kills spontaneity and creativity. Imagination and expansiveness enable a normally functioning person to make creative and coherent choices in order to turn desires into reality. When there is no hope, there are no desires, and life's light turns to eternal darkness.

In order to reverse this disturbing dynamic, one must be able to go to the core of their being and rediscover the forgotten potential within themselves. Desire has to be ignited. A sense of belonging can help, and should be encouraged; family, community, society, humanity – a person needs to feel a connection to something larger than himself. Creating relationships should be supported in order to share with others personal desires and objectives.

A transformation of consciousness, allowing the uncertain and impotent perceptions of self (myself alone) to evolve into degrees of interconnectedness and a sense of community pulls an individual up and out of the murky aloneness of apathy. People who strive to make positive decisions, in their own lives and others', enjoy a sense of possibility, empowerment, spontaneity, creativity ... expressions of self-worth.

To gain control of your own life, you have to be able to control your own mind. It's a process, you make improvements with each positive decision you make. The lower self, the unenlightened, uninquiring, ego-driven part of each of us is like a slave – bound to every passing sensation; whereas, the higher self – true self, strives to a higher level of understanding of the nature of suffering.

You don't want to go through life like a slave, or a clown – like Pagliacci. When things are dragging you down, release them, let them go. Negative thoughts, wrong circumstances, bad influences, unfaithful partners ... all of that has absolutely nothing to do with you! Turn away from the dark and head into the light. Your higher nature understands what's right, and what's right for you. Listen, and do what's right for you!

> If you can't fly, run.
> If you can't run, walk.
> If you can't walk, crawl
> But keep moving forward.
>
> – Martin Luther King, Jr.

Take control of your life, keep moving forward!

OWN YOUR LIFE

To claim complete ownership of your own life – give it away; do something of benefit for others and mankind. The quickest, surest way to reap benefits for yourself is to be completely selfless.

> Alone we can do nothing
> But together our minds fuse into something
> Whose power is far beyond
> The power of its separate parts.
> The kingdom cannot be found alone,
> And you who are the kingdom
> Cannot find yourself alone.
>
> – <u>A Course in Miracles</u>

In Dr. Wayne Dyer's book, <u>The Power of Intention</u>, he writes, "When you eliminate the concept of separation from your thoughts and your behavior, you begin to feel your connection to everything and everyone. You'll begin having a sense of belonging which enables you to scoff at any thought of being separate. How you view others is a projection of how you view yourself. Seeing others as worthless means you're erecting a roadblock for potential allies. Constantly seeing others critically can be a way of compensating for something you fear. If there's a pattern of seeing others as failures, or inferior, that pattern is evidence of what you're attracting into your own life."

Dr. Dyer is a Ph.D. in psychology who has written a long list of books, produced numerous CD's and DVD's, appeared on *Oprah* and several PBS specials. Over the years he's expanded from psychology to spirituality and philosophy.

<u>The Power of Intention</u> is recommended reading for anyone who is trying to improve his life; I put it at the top of the list. Here's a re-telling of an excerpt involving Mother Teresa:

As you're most likely aware, Mother Teresa was a nun who was famous for her selflessness; travelling the world helping humanity and asking for nothing in return. A winner of the Nobel Peace Prize, which includes a significant monetary award, she simply gave it away.

During a radio interview in Phoenix, the interviewer was so taken by her grace and benevolence, he asked what he could do to be of service. Paraphrased here, is her response:

"If you truly want to be of service, I want you to get up tomorrow at four in the morning, go out into the street, and find someone who feels they are all alone, and convince them they aren't."

You see, as Dyer points out, each and every encounter with another human is a holy meeting. By bringing a higher spiritual energy to these encounters you attract a collaboration of higher energies. When the feelings of kindness, love, receptivity and abundance are present in any encounter or relationship, you have brought the spirit of creation into the mix. These forces begin to work in your favor, the right people show up suddenly, the right materials become available, strangers mysteriously appear to help you. Start treating others and doing for others in a divine manner and extraordinary things begin to occur.

Give your life away and more of what you want will magically appear.

KINDNESS

"Simple kindness to one's self and all that lives is the most powerful transformational force of all. It produces no backlash, has no downside, and never leads to loss or despair. It increases one's own true power without exacting any toll. But to reach maximum power such kindness can permit no exceptions, nor can it be practiced with the expectation of some selfish reward. And its effect is as far reaching as it is subtle."

— Dr. David Hawkins
<u>Power vs. Force</u>

There is a vibrational energy to every thought or feeling that you have. Whatever vibrational frequency you're operating within determines how you feel and so many other things. You attract 'like' energies. So when you're down and out and stuck there, guess what? You can expect more of the same. But when you're operating on the high end of the frequency range, you attract similarly high energies back.

Have you ever been engaged in a sporting activity and felt like you were on fire? Like every shot you take is going in, every move you make is easy and sure? Or playing cards or board games, every hand and move is in your favor? You feel a 'buzz', a high like you just can't lose. That's when you're in the zone, riding the high energy wave of positivity and good feelings. That's why they say when you're on a hot streak, ride it out.

Being kind is one of the surest ways to get to that winner's zone. Higher faster energies nullify and convert lower-slower energies.

At some point you're going to need help doing something and the assistance of others will be required. When you're kind to people, attracting the help you need isn't a problem. Think of a boss who is grouchy and tyrannical. His employees are bound to be uncooperative, and how's that play out in the long run? Being unkind to children only makes them want to get back at you, why would they want to help out? To get through life, you're going to need the cooperation of many, many people. If you extend kindness everywhere, to everyone, goodness will come back to you in ways you'd never imagine.

The Jeweler

> If a naïve and desperate man
> Brings a precious stone
> To the only jeweler in town,
> Wanting to sell it,
> The jeweler's eyes
> Will begin to play a game,
> Like most eyes in the world when they look at you.
>
> The jeweler's face will stay calm.
> He will not want to reveal the stone's true value,
> But to hold the man captive to fear and greed
> While he calculates
> The value of the transaction.
>
> But one moment with me, my dear,
> Will show you that there is nothing Hafiz wants from you.
> When you sit before a Master like me,
> Even if you are a drooling mess,
> My eyes will sing with Excitement.
> They will see your Divine worth.
>
> — Hafiz

When you are kind to people, even when you don't know them and even without understanding the dynamics of the universe at large, good things will happen in your own life. If you are kind ALL THE TIME, imagine what might occur? What you give out is what you will receive back. Serve, and thou shall be served.

If you understand these dynamics, you can begin to control your environment. Since every thought in your head has an energy to it which will either strengthen or weaken you, it is obvious you should make efforts to eliminate the lower energies while enhancing the highs. Being kind is the most important thing you can do to instantly make your life better.

Think about it. If you're kind to everyone and everything, including yourself, and life gives back to you what you put out – you can expect wonderful things back. Of course, no matter what, we all have tragedies and occurrences that are painful and unpleasant. But, if you understand that every circumstance in life is a lesson, and try to understand what may be learned from disagreeable events, you can face life with head held high and not allow circumstances to dictate how to approach your life.

Have you ever heard the dictum: If you go through life looking for ways to be upset, life will not disappoint you? The converse is the same. If you are kind, and look for goodness and beauty everywhere, you won't be disappointed. You cannot see outside of you what you fail to see within.

The concept of extending kindness is especially relevant in how you deal with the elderly, mentally challenged, poor, disabled, helpless, etc., as all these types of people are a part of the perfection of the universe and connected to you (and everyone else) just as surely as your arm is connected to your shoulder. Just because someone is different than you or your family or friends, doesn't make them 'less'. In fact, have you considered that at times perhaps the universe puts someone different in your path just to see how you might react.

ENDLESS LOVE

"The love we take, is equal to the love we make."

– Lennon & McCartney

"Compassion is the highest moral value, the noblest human feeling, the purest love. It is the final social expression of man's divinity. For he is able to feel with and for another only because both are in reality related in harmony by the presence of that soul in each other."

— Paul Brunton, philosopher

How often do we hear the word 'love' spoken? Many times a day, perhaps, and its various meanings and degrees range from a subtle fondness to the greatest truth one can know. We cherish love as an ultimate value and devote ourselves to becoming more loving. Even though we may experience this feeling, many times we may wonder, what is love, actually? Where does it come from?

The Chinese mystic Lao-tzu taught: "He who knows, tells it not; he who tells, knows it not."

Love's meaning and origin resides within each and every one of us, seek inward to find the mysteries of the unanswerable. When a child looks upon its mother for the first time, the love there is so pure and unquestionable as to be undeniable. It is this brand and quality of love that we devote an entire lifetime to finding and acquiring, looking in all the dark corners and twisting avenues, seldom to ever regain what was lost in the innocence of childhood.

We've become perverse in our quest for love. The experience of love between two hearts, is perhaps the closest thing to the ultimate experience of a divine love between heart and soul. And, as humans, we many times end our searching when we find that bond that, for a time, fulfills the basic need. That's why we tend to be on the lookout for that signal, the eye of another who recognizes similar needs.

And, so often we settle for poor substitutes, confused that sex, money, material gain, fame, notoriety, even the momentary high of a drug rush, somehow equate to that which we innately seek. Ultimate love.

None of those outward forces can quench the unquenchable thirst. It's only through study, sacrifice and higher awareness that we can begin to experience pure love. The passage from the common animalistic behavior to spiritual humanity requires a raising of force and focus from the generative organ to the thinking one. Or, in the common vernacular, "We need to start thinking with the other head". To progress, to experience higher love, that which up to now has be externalized must be internalized; what was wasted must be conserved, and what has been physically spent must be spiritually transformed.

The incarcerated are in a uniquely contrived environment to begin to make this progression from the sensual to the sublime. Because the other sex is, in most cases, on the other side of that fence and, for the most part, unattainable, we can begin using the pent up energies we're used to using in the quest for a physical manifestation of desires, and turn it inward. Ironically, the inability to satiate the base urges can force us to seek a higher satisfaction. Divine love.

I'm not talking about religion, even though the religious espouse the same quest theologically. I'm talking about getting in touch and in tune with the same energy that created you and all of us and everything, and keeps the whole dynamic perpetuating on and on. It is metaphysical and so immense that it's nearly incomprehensible. Which really makes Lao-tzu appear that much wiser, because it's so colossal, it can't be described in words.

You know that feeling you get when you meet that special one? And instantly you feel that it was meant to be and there has to be something bigger out there contriving to bring you two together? Well, all that's true.

And, if you take that feeling you have for that special one and multiply it by ten-thousand, you'll 'begin' to start to conceive the kind of love that's available to you by opening up your heart and mind to the infinite power and possibilities that are within your grasp, IF you allow it!

I understand that the easy thing to do is take it as it comes, and if what you've been doing up to this point is working for you, why mess with it? But the problem is, it hasn't been working, has it? And now that you've been made aware there's something greater out there, how are you ever going to be satisfied with the same old same old?

We're talking about illumination here, and the price you pay to gain access is self-surrender. Anyone can gain entrance to the understanding, but the price is to leave doubt and ego behind, a change of attitude to one of acceptance that there is within you a higher awareness that can only be accessed by rising above your lower nature. Our imperfections will remain, but through them the light of knowing shines.

To find this love, to attain this height, we have to sacrifice our lower emotions on the altar of the quest. Anger, greed, lust, aggressive egoism, any of the ugly, repellant reactive learned mechanisms and manifestations of human frailty, burned and discarded in the fire of the authentic urge for self-improvement and quest for the higher self.

Every time we crush out a wrong or foolish thought, we add to our inner strength. Every time we bravely face up to misfortune with calm appraisal of the lesson presented, we add to our inner wisdom. The man who wisely and self-critically surrenders himself may proceed forward with a sense of security and assurance, hopeful and unafraid, because he is being guarded by his own higher nature. If we have taken the trouble to understand intellectually the lessons that adversity provides for us, we may then conquer the evils of life. When faced with situations that heretofore have caused us to swoon or bend our will, and at the onset, turn inward and realize that our divinity within allows us the power, knowledge, and ability to withstand and conquer, then we have found harmony of self and the greater powers of nature and source.

The love in our heart, untainted by lower nature, has the power to supersede any adversity! If we may know this, if we may comprehend the concept, how could we ever be daunted by the minor travails of life?

Doubt, fear, anxiety, the dark forces of a cowardly lower nature … banished by the greatest emotion – love.

"E lucevan le stele"

Puccini: Tosca (Act III)

> And the stars were shining … the earth
> smelt sweet … the garden gate creaked …
> and a footstep brushed the sand.
> She entered, fragrant,
> and fell into my arms.
> O soft kisses, tender caresses,
> while I, all a quiver,
> unveiled her lovely features!
> Vanished forever is my dream of love …
> That time has fled
> and I die in despair.
> Never have I loved life so dearly!

As is Italian opera, so is life. Revealed many times between the lines, said without saying. The 'she' entering through the garden gate, is death. He waited too long to discover love, and now … too late.

Don't live the tragic dilemma, discover the love within yourself and share it … in every situation, to all who come within your reach. The secret lies within your reach, the key to the universe awaits. In the midst of tragedy and poverty you may claim the greatest joy and wealth, the love in your own heart

HAS LOVE
(review)

H – Honesty. With yourself and others. Own up to your past and face your future. The very first thing you must do to improve is to be honest!

A – Ask forgiveness and forgive those who have hurt you. If you want to be forgiven, you must forgive. It is a great burden off your shoulders, and a test of your courage.

S – Seek your soul. Search inside and find the goodness from which you came. You are part of a great consciousness and interconnectedness. Discover your soul and you will know your higher nature.

L – Live under control. Your thoughts, emotions, words, actions … if you aren't controlling them, who is? To have a good life, you must take control.

O – Own your life by giving it away. Do for others, live for others' benefit. Only by giving do you receive.

V – Voice kindness, be the voice of kindness. Think, speak, act in a kind manner and show kindness to all equally. Everyone has a divine nature and is as deserving as the next.

E – Endless love. Strive to discover your higher nature and find the love you are capable of achieving and sharing. Exploring this highest degree of awareness, love puts us on the path to true enlightenment.

CHAPTER SIX: THE CAULDRON OF ADVERSITY

On our way to personal reform, revision and rehabilitation, we're tested. Our characters are forged and strengthened through adversity, we become stronger every time we face up to circumstances that are borne to wither and wear away at our beings. In the interest of candor, herein I share with you one of my own episodes of adversity.

The First O.J. Book

I got the idea for an O.J. Simpson book long before all the others came out. The inspiration came in a flash at three in the morning as I lay awake on 'B' row in L.A. County Jail's Highpower, 1700. The only sounds on the row of 25 one-man cells were cockroaches scurrying across the concrete floor ... the same floor worn smooth by the thousands, perhaps millions of feet that have tread there. I was certain that I wasn't the only one in Highpower that wasn't able to sleep that night.

Over on 'G' row the Juice had to be having at least a twinge of remorse. That's because this was, exactly to the day, the one-year anniversary of the death of Nicole Brown Simpson and Ron Goldman. It wasn't O.J.'s problems that were keeping me awake, however. By coincidence, it happened to be my wedding anniversary. I'd lost my wife and kids when I'd gotten myself arrested a year before, and I was considering how a guy could get himself so screwed up and leave such a horrendous trail of heartbreak and sorrow in his wake.

All that made me think of O.J., and that's when it dawned on me that I was in the perfect position to write the very first, original, and now – long lost and forgotten – O.J. Book. I used to be a reporter, mostly for an all-news radio station in Miami, WINZ NEWS. Crime beat stuff, show up at a crime scene or car wreck, murders, coke busts, political news conferences, pretty boring fare, really. I was just biding my time until I could fulfill my real dream – disc jockey. (That turned out to be a bust, though. Come to find out, spinning the same records over and over, no matter how cool it seemed at the time, is beyond monotonous. I should have stuck with the news.)

One of the good things about working around a newsroom is, you learn a lot. Twenty-four-seven the wire services are feeding news over the teletype. One line blurbs, three line headlines, five page in-depth feature stories. Unusual words, places and names are phonetically spelled out, background information is available within minutes, it was the Internet before the net existed. I was doing the midnight to six A.M. anchor shift when John Lennon and Elvis died. I got the inside skinny on Ted Bundy and Son of Sam. I learned how to write, what leads, and what the professionals consider newsworthy. When you're around that atmosphere for a while you get a sense of what's interesting to the public. If it bleeds, it leads, isn't just a newsroom slogan, it's a newsman's credo. And on this special occasion, Nicole and Ron's blood was still warm and dripping all over the *L.A. Times* and every other local and national newscast across the country and the world. The trial was being broadcast in real time, live, all day long. We were watching it on the rows. The defense was brilliant, the prosecution pathetic, and the drama dynamic. And, I knew exactly how I could make it all work for me.

I'd write not only about O.J. and the trial, but also about the inside story of the inner workings of L.A. County Jail's Highpower, and what really goes on with the Juice, and everybody else, inside. The real deal about the belly of the beast. And there was the title: "Deep Inside the Belly of the Beast." I'd use the profits from book sales to finance my own legal defense. At the time, I didn't have a lawyer, not a real one, that is. I promise you, the only justice you or anybody else is going to get in L.A. is equal to what you can pay for, no exaggeration. I've seen guys who weren't even remotely guilty get life, or worse. Others walk free, trailing the blood of their victims behind. O.J. did a county year for double-murder.

By dumb luck I was in a unique position to work this project. I was right up front on 'B' row and able to see everyone who came or went from Highpower. There are seven Highpower rows in 1700 - 1750. 'A' through 'C' are mainline, 'D' and 'E' are processing, or orientation, 'F' and 'G' are special needs, like protective custody or super-high profile. O.J. had all of 'G' row, that's right, the whole row of 25 one-man cells, to himself.

That was for his safety. Believe me, there are dudes over there who wouldn't think twice about making a name for themselves as being the guy who snuffed the Juice. I'm not saying it would be easy, O.J. ain't no punk, the guy was a leading NFL running back and nearly carried the Buffalo Bills to the Superbowl on his back. But those guys in Highpower can be treacherous and if they want to get you, they'll find a way. You learn quickly to keep your mouth shut and your eyes open. To survive Highpower you learn all about respect, how to give it and get it.

Another windfall bonus to my location was that I could see right into the guard's control booth and on the desk was a five-inch video monitor of O.J.'s cell. He had an exercise bike over there! Every night when he got back from court they had big pitchers of orange juice and ice water waiting for him and food from the officer's dining room. I remember one time, it was Christmas or Thanksgiving, the Lieutenant came rolling into the unit and announced, "Go get O.J. a big plate of fried chicken from ODR." They sent the most red-neckedest, tobacco chewingest, Klan-meeting attendingest guard there was to go fetch O.J. some chicken. He was NOT happy about it, either, and they all had a good laugh. Jail is the most segregated and hardcore racist sub-society you'll ever encounter. But O.J. was a football hero and a celebrity. He was cock-of-the-walk, rook-of-the-roost. The Juice was treated extremely well. It was this dichotomy between his treatment and the way the rest of us were treated, that led me to believe that a real life, behind the scenes story would be interesting, and a best seller.

I began writing and taking careful notice of every move O.J. made. He was in court nearly every day, and non-court days he spent in the visiting room where he had his own booth. He and Shapiro and the blonde assistant would be out there all day long. I knew it was probably because he couldn't stand being in that cell, even if he did have the whole tier to himself. He was escorted by five guards, coming or going anywhere he went. Occasionally, we'd pass in the entry way. The guy's got a presence about him. Energy sparks off this dude like lightning bolts hitting a transformer in an electrical storm. He's physically imposing, about six-three, still in good shape in 1994, a huge head, and he'd stare you down.

Seeing the guy standing there waiting to go to court, it was easy to conceive how he brutalized Nicole and Ron. He made a career speeding around, past or through two hundred fifty pound linebackers, and was accustomed to slamming into tree hundred plus pound defensive linemen to be a leading NFL rusher year after year. A couple of Brentwood socialites are no competition. That's like a lawnmower through a daisy patch. One time, Juice came back from court and noticed I'd hung up that big cover shot of Nicole from the *National Enquirer* on my cell wall, right where he could see it. I thought he was going to come through the Plexiglas. Honestly, he rushed up to the glass and played it off like he was trying to get the basketball playoff score from the TV, but he was livid, and even in handcuffs, a maniac.

I began calling around to the Century City attorneys. I'd get them to come visit by feigning interest in their representing me on my case. Although that was partly true, the first priority was finding someone connected well enough to get an O.J. book brokered. And, it had to be someone who understood the potential. I found a well-known, very expensive attorney that was willing to work with me. I could wrap the manuscript fairly quickly, get it to him and he'd handle the rest. Within days he was back with an offer based solely on the concept I'd presented verbally to him. It was from a tabloid, though, a hundred thousand for the story, and, they wanted pictures. They wanted to slip me a miniature camera, and even offered bribe money to get a guard to take shots of O.J.'s cell or even O.J. himself. It was doable, all the obstacles could be overcome. I could get the camera back to the unit, take pictures myself from the cell, even bribe the overnight guard and get it all back out. Only one thing would prevent the deal from going through – me. I turned it down. I was holding out for the book deal, the numbers were too tempting. On a book that would sell for upwards of twenty dollars a pop, figuring that it is easily a million-seller, that's twenty mil. The author gets ten to fifteen percent, that's two to three million. And the kind of money I would need in order to pay off the attorney and buy my way out. The lawyer saw it too, we agreed to hold out for the book deal and I got back to work.

Juice was back and forth to court, the TV coverage was overwhelming and free advertising for the book. I was interweaving stories of jailhouse exploits and the horrors of being inside, with the O.J. story. I'd been in seven full-blown riots, seen guys get stabbed and sliced, witnessed dead bodies dragged out, seen and/or been involved in illicit romances involving guards, nurses, lawyers, or girlfriends hired as 'legal assistants'. The lawyers would bring them to court where they'd meet privately with the prisoner in a holding cell for 'legal conferencing'. Yeah, that stuff goes on. I've known of deals where judges traded sex for sweet deals. One guy on our row had his wife visit a judge, the guy got so hooked on the woman that he tried to put the husband away forever so he could keep the wife. It was all over the news.

When cigarettes were banned from jail and prison it created a black market that rivaled alcohol prohibition from the 1920's. Suddenly, a pack of cigarettes could be broken down and sold in tiny pieces that netted $240.00 a pack! That's better mark-up than anything I've seen on the NYSE … and the profit on heroin is even more staggering. I've actually heard guards get on the intercom to the rows on visiting day and announce to certain inmates the amounts that were credited to their account by a visitor (of other inmates.)

The guards were literally advising the drug dealer that his buyers had paid, or not, which meant a client whose people hadn't dropped off money to his account could be in serious trouble. Remember, this is the Mexican Mafia and very serious people are involved. Even the guards were scared of them. There were times when two cell doors were 'accidentally' opened on the tier at the same time. It was common knowledge that when that occurred you were supposed to 'deal with it'.

All of this going on was an incredibly fertile field of interesting characters, back stories, and circumstances from which I could harvest genuine drama for the book. Hardened gang members, grizzled guards, rich attorneys, ambitious prosecutors, corrupt judges. Mix in sex and violence, money and greed, politics and a celebrity double-murder ... not only the case of the century, but a can't miss best seller! What could possibly go wrong?

When they showed up at my cell door fifteen deep in riot gear, I knew the jig was up and I was the one getting the jag. Somehow, the jail administrators caught wind of my little project. Not the tabloid offer and the camera smuggling, just the writing end. But that was enough to unleash a response worthy of comparison to the seven plagues of Egypt. The SWAT crew gaffed me up and swept me away to the darkest, dankest, most desolate far corner of the jail, and as far away from O.J. as they could get me. Highpower overflow. Twenty five cells of one-man cages on the third floor, mice and rats roaming at will in the thousands and nothing but crazies and hardcore program failures. There was a good inch of water on the floor, I got a shower about every twelve days. And you could forget about phone calls or rec time or civil rights.

I was in the last cell on the last tier. When they cell fed, if they ran out of trays – they weren't coming back. I used stubs of pencil and tore away the wood around the lead by gnawing with my teeth or chipping with fingernails. Any scrap of paper I could get my hands on I wrote on. For the next thirty days, I wrote. There was absolutely nothing else to do anyway. I was so weak from hunger and neglect that all I wanted to do was sleep. Depression was a constant threat, and I fought it off long enough to get the manuscript done.

My investigator came for a visit and I slipped it to him with instructions to get it to the attorney to get it typed, edited and dealt to a publisher. Two weeks later I saw the investigator again and I asked how it went. He replied, "Oh, that was a really good story!" I was taken aback because I was very clear that it was urgent to get it to the lawyer ASAP. My response was, "You read it?" The alarm bells began blaring when he answered, "Yeah, I'm a bit of a writer, myself." He'd submitted some of his work to *Reader's Digest* but had gotten rejected.

Now the alarms in my head were going off like those big steel ones they use in school auditoriums to signal some imminent disaster, like hurricanes or nuclear bomb attacks. I struggled to remain calm and politely inquired if he might possibly be sure to get the manuscript to the attorney as soon as possible. It's important. He assured me it would be done. A year and three court orders later, the investigator was forced to hand over my hand-written manuscript in court. I'm pretty sure he sold the story to one of the tabloids, I had read one that the attorney showed me that seemed very similar. They had used some really fake studio composite cut and paste to represent O.J.'s cell, it was really tacky.

But by that time it didn't matter, anyway. The trial of the century had ended, everybody and their neighbor's brother had written an O.J. book and my window of opportunity had slammed shut, been double-secured with those locks they shoot rifle bullets through, and laser-welded tight, with me inside.

I read all the other books; Clark, Darden, Bugliosi, and others. None of them came close to the drama of actually being inside, living in the same unit with the Juice. It was all very anti-climactic. I got myself moved over to the Pro-Per side, with all the other guys representing themselves. At least I got out of exile and could go to the law library for an hour or two a day. The verdict was a surprise to us on the inside. We thought it would be a hung jury, re-trial, conviction. Looking back, it was a masterful job by

Johnny Cochran. Regardless how you feel about guilt or innocence, you hope that if you ever find yourself in dire legal circumstances, someone would fight so diligently for your freedom. It's rare.

I've moved on since those days, to state prison. Pursued other writing projects, spent a lot of time on self-discovery and improvement. Ironically, although The First O.J. Book was never published, the essay on the writing of it won the national PEN Writing Awards competition and was a catalyst for my other writings. O.J. went on and did his thing for a while in Florida, then Vegas. Maybe we do all get what we deserve, ultimately. Six, seven, eight books later, I'm still at it, and appreciate that the adversity faced has provided me with a wellspring of invaluable material.

Looking back, reliving the events from over twenty years ago in these pages, it's still so vivid and clear … and bizarre. The oddest part is, every word is true.

You meet some guys in here who have stories of overcoming adversity that make my own seem tame. For instance, Coco. Here's a guy who is one of the nicest, most well-mannered and decent people you could ever meet. I'm always looking for interesting back stories for book characters so when I asked him about his own history, what he told me was so unique, I knew I'd eventually use it … with Coco's permission, of course.

When Coco was quite young, his mother and father divorced and he and his older brother went with the mother. She soon pawned them off to another relative in the state of Maine. One day, when Coco and his brother came home from school, they discovered that the relative had moved. Yes, completely moved away, no forwarding address! Coco was about ten years old, the brother, closer to seventeen.

For the next weeks they carried on as well as they could, not letting on that there were no adults about. They took to shoplifting in order to survive. One of their favorite targets was a truck stop gift shop where they'd steal food. Soon, however, the apartment manager caught on and told them he'd have to report them to the authorities. That's when difficult circumstances turned dire for Coco. The brother announced that he'd met a truck driver who was willing to take Coco with him and look after him. A complete stranger, and strange doesn't begin to describe it.

For the next five years, Coco was held captive in a diesel truck, chained up and used as a sex slave. Come to find out, there's a whole network of cross-country truckers who engage in some really pervo-freaky stuff. They meet up with one another along the truck routes for orgies and kid-trading. Many of them have runaways or captives or just maladjusted youngsters riding along. They use drugs, alcohol, abuse and torture to control them. Coco withstood this for five years before being rescued in an FBI sting. I read the actual transcripts of the depositions. Who even knew this was going on? Now, when I see stories on the news about truckers being involved in serial killings, it's not such a surprise.

A lot of the guys that end up in here have some amazingly bizarre childhoods. I used to eat breakfast with a really quiet guy who always kept to himself and didn't bother anybody. Robert was a very soft-spoken, respectful person. He was also a serial-killer. Come to find out, he'd made a deal to show them where the bodies were in order to avoid the chair, and he didn't mind talking about it.

Robert grew up in the backwoods of Mississippi, way back in the woods. When he was twelve years old he got his first kill. He and a friend were playing army, Robert was using a .22 rifle and accidentally scored a kill shot on his buddy. He ran home and told his mama, who responded by shaking him and saying, "You don't never talk about this again!" In those parts of Mississippi, one less mouth to feed isn't necessarily a cause for mourning or investigation by the authorities, especially in the early 1960's when poor black folks kept to themselves and out of the eye of white law enforcement.

When he and his mother moved to Los Angeles and Robert found himself in the middle of civil rights' riots he took the opportunity to score even more anonymous kills. He told me, "I enjoyed it."

Over breakfast for the next few weeks, Robert told me about a string of murders that ran all the way from that first one at age twelve, well into his forties. The guy stands about 6'7" and could easily twist a neck or pummel someone to death. The fact that he liked what he'd done was that much more macabre. I soon realized that he would serve well as the inspiration for the most evil, vile villain of the book I was writing at the time, <u>Goodbye Natalie</u>. All the killings and scenes of carnage by the deadly Mississippi Mudcat Jones in <u>Goodbye Natalie</u> are based on Robert's string of murders, with his permission, of course.

You see old guys like Robert wandering these dayrooms and walking the track and they don't strike you as anyone dangerous. But, looks can be deceiving. It's been said that the experiences of life ennoble some people but degrade others, and in the end affect our thoughts, desires, and feelings only as we let them. It is our choice, ultimately, to say whether they shall call forth our divinity or our brutality. Our attitude of mind helps determine our experience of the world.

When we're brought to bear the consequences of our wrongs, it is human to prefer to avoid the suffering, or at least to diminish it. We can help to modify or ameliorate the consequences if we set into motion certain counteracting influences. First, we have to take to heart deeply the lessons of our wrongs and blame no one and nothing outside of ourselves, our own moral weaknesses and mental infirmities and allow no self-deception. We should feel the pangs of remorse and constant thoughts of repentance.

Next, we must harbor no ill feelings against anyone for whatever reason. Third, we must think continuously and head directly in the opposite direction of our wrong-doing. Fourth, swear a personal oath to never again commit such wrongs. This has to be heart-felt, deeply meant, and renewed frequently. This is where you go deep inside yourself and find that place where your true inner spirit dwells, and commune there. Delve into those depths, seek guidance, solace, forgiveness and inspiration from within.

If you're headed anywhere in life that's good, then the painful experiences and adversities are serving as lessons, and there are valuable things to be learned there. We learn more from suffering than we do from pleasure. What happens to us is significant, but what we make of it, is paramount.

The very type of experience which man most dislikes to have is the very kind which forces him to contemplate its cause, and begin, even unknowingly, to search for the deeper meaning of life. Disappointments in emotional life, suffering physical maladies, misfortunes in personal affairs should teach us to discriminate more carefully, to examine more thoroughly, and have more empathy for those who also bear sorrow.

Failures in life, in career, relationships, lost opportunities, wrong choices aren't necessarily wasted effort. From each situation we can salvage the tuition for a fresh start, build a foundation of wisdom and self-knowledge that pays dividends, not only for ourselves, but all others around us.

It's the adversity we've faced that has made us who we are today, someone better than yesterday, and not as good as tomorrow. Someone we would be proud to share with others.

In closing this chapter I would like to share with you a story that's one of my favorites. It's from L.A. County and involves one of my best friends, Bandit.

At the time, Bandit was 22 years old, facing the death penalty for a double murder. The best jailhouse lawyers looked at his case to try and find wiggle room, there wasn't any, it was airtight. Bandit was going down and nothing was going to prevent it. But, the guy was still a happy, upbeat individual, a spark of energy in a really drab environment. He lifted all our spirits.

One night I asked him how he kept himself so jovial, considering what he was facing. He was quiet for a moment, then slid his arm through the bars from the next cell and handed me a folded up picture from a magazine. In the picture was this little black African baby. It had a distended stomach from starvation and its head was drooping, eyes half-closed as he or she sat in the dirt. Off to the side in the background, a vulture stood by, waiting.

Bandit told me that whenever ho got to feeling sorry for himself, he pulled out that picture and looked at it.

We all go through adversity in life, some of us more than others. And, no matter what ours may be, somebody's always got it worse. The important thing is, if we can live through it, learn from it, and become better, more compassionate human beings, maybe it's all worth it.

D. Razor Babb

CHAPTER SEVEN: MEDITATION

"All creative scientists know that the true laboratory is the mind."

– J.C. Bose, Indian scientist

The real secret to living well, to self-improvement, to fulfillment … is that there is much to be learned from books, teachers, the Internet, and all other outside influences – but the truth of ultimate revelation is only learned from within oneself … through meditation.

And it's not hocus-pocus, simply deep contemplation that can be enhanced by focused attention. One of the most valuable aspects of meditation is that it carries consciousness down to a deeper level, allowing a person to live from his center, not the surface alone. The result being that we are then not dominated by mere physical sense-reactions, like animals, but a mind that begins to expand, employing greater self-control, self-awareness and higher awareness.

If you are thinking and reacting from a limited consciousness that is dictated by normal sense perception, this is surface awareness, also known as shallowness. A person operating from a shallow perspective can never know depth of nature, character, thought. Only from the depths of our inner selves, and by becoming aware of something greater than 'self', may we begin to experience a deeper consciousness, depth of nature.

A person can be smart, educated, even successful, but still be shallow.

Conversely, a person can be uneducated, even illiterate, poor and socially unsuccessful, yet, have depth. What's really interesting about deeper consciousness, is that anyone can delve into it. If you look into your heart and mind intently enough, you can penetrate beneath the distractions of day-to-day living and the common rush of desires that constantly tug our attention away from larger, more fulfilling introspection. Beyond the rattle and hum of money and rum lies the peace of an inner world beyond our wildest imagining.

Have you ever considered where Einstein came up with the theory of relativity? I mean, there were no books that taught that concept, it was beyond the knowledge available in the earthly world. How about the first people to harness electricity? Or send radio waves? All great inventions or ideas come in the form of a hunch. A thought suddenly placed or recognized in the mind that comes from where? Well, they come from 'out there'. Not exactly the explanation you're looking for? OK, I'll try to narrow it down.

Beyond the normal consciousness of a single mind, is a greater expanse of 'thought'. Your brain works on electricity. We're made up of atoms, which have a nucleus of protons and neutrons, with electrons spinning around the center. Our spinal column transfers electrons up and down, distributing messages and orders through our body from the brain. Involuntary and voluntary commands. Up in the brain, constant electronic stimulus is circulating away, resulting in physical, mental, emotional reactions.

Now, outside of our bodies, exists a whole expansive realm of energy, atoms, and matter of which atoms are made, that is in constant flux, keeping the planets revolving and the galaxies in order. All that energy bumping around is a part of the same energy that we each operate on. It is all interconnected and happening this very moment. It's known by various titles or words; here, for the sake of inclusion, we'll call it 'universal energy'. Within this universal energy everything that ever was or ever will be, exists. Even 'thought'. The deep thoughts that brought Einstein the information he needed to come up with $E = MC2$, came out of the ether of universal energy.

When you have a 'hunch', it is coming from that expansive ether of the universal energy, out there. Have you ever been riding along in the car and started singing a song, then turned on the radio and that song was playing? Have you ever wondered how that occurred? The radio waves that are traveling through the ether were picked up by the electronic energy in your brain, your consciousness and uber-consciousness, allowing you to 'hear' that song playing before you even turned the radio on. How about when you pick up the phone to call someone and there they are, already on the line. The electrical energy in your mind sent out waves that the other person picked up on, or, theirs were picked up by you.

This is where meditation comes in. By quieting your mind, letting the leaves of wandering thoughts settle and drift to the ground, you can tune in to the deeper thoughts that that are available to anyone, if they'd just listen.

Any answer to any question you have is available through meditation. You can tap into that great universal energy by relaxing, clearing you head of distracting thoughts, being quiet and zoning in to the great expanse. Anybody can do it.

The best way to begin is by sitting or standing with your spine straight, so the electrical energy can surge freely. Relax your muscles, let all the random thoughts fall away, focus on the spot where your spine meets your brain (it's located directly behind the space between your eyes), now breathe in deeply, give it four or five counts, hold it, let it out slowly. Do this over and over, relaxing your body again and again, focusing on the spot between your eyes, breathing slowly and deeply.

Random thoughts are going to creep in, push them away. Thinking of something pleasant may help, like visualizing the sun or a cloud. Keep breathing slowly and deeply until you're completely relaxed. Now, if you have a problem or issue you need to resolve, put that thought into your mind, ask the question or just think of the point you need to ponder, then let it go. Breathe, relax, let the answer come. It will, it always does – if we're not listening though, we can't hear the answer.

That's meditation, easy as that. Of course, there are degrees of the practice. You can go for two minutes, two hours, or two to two hundred days depending on your desire and ability. Hindu swamis or Tibetan monks go on and on and on, we're not quite there, yet. I can promise you, though, if you try this and give it an honest effort, you will experience results.

When I got off that Highpower overflow row and onto the Pro-Per side, that's when I discovered meditation. Joe Hunt was over there, and all the way into it. I mean, he was so intent on meditation that every time I passed his cell he was in the lotus position and practically humming with energy. He was so peaceful and self-aware and in-tune with everything, I couldn't help but wonder what his secret was. He handed me a book, Autobiography of a Yogi, by Paramahansa Yogananda, and there was no looking back from there.

Yogananda lived 1893 to 1952, and is the originating force behind the Self-Realization Fellowship organization, and widely known for bringing esoteric teachings of the East to the West. He migrated to America in 1920, and brought a revealing look of the Hindu mind and heart to this continent. He knew from a very young age that he was meant to be a yogi, and insistently followed the path all his life; he is known as one of the preeminent spiritualists of the twentieth century. His book has been translated into eighteen languages and serves as a profound introduction to the science and philosophy of yoga, revealing the underlying unity of the great religions of the world.

For me, it was a revelation. Once I began meditating, everything suddenly became clear. Everything I'd been doing up to that point was wrong. I thought I was the one in control of my life, how wrong that turned out to be. There was something so much greater and bigger at work, and I'd been ignorant of it my entire life! I started meditating for a few moments, then longer … and longer. At the height of it I was in a trance for four and five hours at a time; this in the L.A. County Jail, the dirtiest, scurviest, meanest place on earth! And here I was, experiencing bliss for the first time ever.

You go into those long trances and you discover stuff you can only barely imagine. Answers suddenly began to come, understanding of self and others, even complex issues that I couldn't have begun to conceive before, were now within my grasp.

At the height of my meditative indoctrination I took a three strikes case to trial, pro-per, facing 25-to-life on it. I got a 'not guilty'.

To appreciate the extreme difficulty and unlikelihood of successfully executing a jury trial you have to be aware of the numbers. The conviction rate for regular cases, ones where defendants have an attorney, in L.A. County is in the high 80 percentile range. Cases where guys represent themselves are in the 99.99 percent range. It's rare.

I never planned on taking any case to trial on my own. The pro-per case was one that I had picked up in jail and only went pro-per to reap the benefits of the law library and the little perks that come with the status.

After messing around with it for many, many months, my judge got irritated and forced me into trial, generously allowing me 30 days to prepare. If not for Joe Hunt and meditation, I'd have gotten 25-to-life on that case, I have no doubt.

Early on in my confinement I'd been found in possession of a hacksaw blade at court. It was a clumsy escape attempt, and ill-advised. I was caught red-handed with a hacksaw blade in my legal folder. Possession of an instrument to aid in an escape is a felony, in my case, a third felony ... strike three, which equals 25-to-life. I figured since it was a jailhouse case I'd just pro-per it, and see how the main case went. If I lost that, the other one wouldn't matter. If I won the original case I'd hand the hacksaw thing over to a real attorney. So much for the master plan.

Anyway, there I was, surrounded by the assistant D.A., all the forces of the L.A. County District Attorney's Office, and a courtroom famous for quick convictions. Being caught with the thing in my folder seemed like a slam dunk for the A.D.A., and she knew it. Everybody in court knew it. Even me.

But, somehow the universe was providing. Joe Hunt happened to be one of the most capable legal minds in the country, and he convinced me I had a chance. He had all the legal books I'd need; opening and closing arguments, rules of evidence, direct and cross examination, objections, jury selection, all of it. I studied ten hours a day and wrote the whole trial out like it was a play, including the ending. I was meditating about four hours a day and I've never been more focused on anything in my entire life, or better prepared.

It was me and a yellow legal tablet and #2 pencil versus the really experienced A.D.A., and all her friends and associates. I was severely out-gunned and it was obvious from the start. I spent four days on jury selection. She kept dismissing the blacks, I kept arguing for their selection. By the time opening statements began, they were starting to warm up to me. But just as I began my statement, she jumped in with the objections and it looked like my inexperience would be the end of me. They say anyone who represents himself has a fool for a client. Well, I was out to prove there wasn't anyone more foolish than me.

I finally got through the opening argument and the prosecution's case began. She had detectives, correctional officers, expert witnesses, forensic analysts, and every other thing you might dream of. The case was so airtight, I would have probably voted for conviction, it was that convincing. Her only real error was, in her enthusiasm to win she was willing to go above and beyond the limits of where the evidence took her, she was willing to lie.

Not that she planned it that way, but in the course of the trial she made a judgment call that was fatal to the case. The crux of my case was reasonable doubt, that there was a possibility that even though I was found to have been holding a legal folder with a hacksaw blade in it; it was 'possible' I didn't know it was in there. A huge stretch of imagination for any jury member, but it was all I had. I was trying to call witnesses down from state prison (who had been in court that day) to testify the blade may have belonged to someone else. But, the A.D.A. thwarted my efforts to retain those witnesses, so I had to work around it.

There had been massive race riots going on throughout the county jail and prison system during that time. It was my position that, as a result of the tension, a riot kicked off at court that day in the holding cells and all our property, including legal folders, got mixed up. I simply picked up the wrong one. In fact, it was true that a riot had occurred at court that day, so my scenario had some validity to it. At least it was an argument for reasonable doubt.

Still, she had all her witnesses, and credibility and righteousness ... and the blade. Oh, wait, no blade. It was missing from evidence. What? "Ladies and gentlemen of the jury, I beseech you. How can we send a guy away for life ..."

"Objection!"

"Sustained. You can't tell the jury the sentence you're facing."

They brought the jail maintenance man in to tell them how he used the thing, "It was in there for so long, I figured I'd use it ...."

She showed them an exact duplicate of the blade, "Objection. Is this the actual blade you're saying I had in my possession? No? Just checking."

No worries, everybody just calm down, you CAN present replacement evidence for evidence lost. Whew, that was close. But now, for some reason I still don't fully understand, the prosecution's case takes an odd twist. They're insisting that my whole defense is in error, and nothing but smoke and mirrors because – THERE WAS NO RIOT IN COURT THAT DAY!

What? Are you kidding me? I couldn't believe it. Each and every witness, one after another testified that there was no riot, no tension, it was just another pleasant day in court and jail. They were going to tow that hard line that I was making it all up. And since they had prevented me from presenting witnesses, and I wasn't going to testify (Because that meant revealing my own criminal history) who was going to doubt the word of police, investigators, correctional officers, and the integrity of the L.A. District Attorney's Office?

They almost got away with it. Not only that, since their lie was holding up, they got emboldened. They had the jail bus driver testify that somebody told him, before we arrived at court, that I had a blade. Really? And, thank you. "Officer Goldstar, (not his real name) when you were advised that I was in possession of a hacksaw blade on the bus, what did you do?"

"I told the guards at court."

"And what about the racial tension and rioting?"

"No tension, no riots."

I presented log entries from the L.A. County Jail that documented the rioting from that day. And, courthouse log entries for that date. No report from Officer Goldstar, and no reports of rioting (the rioting had been expunged from the courthouse holding cell logs.)

They were caught in a lie, and if they're going to lie about that, what else are they lying about and what lengths will they go to for a conviction? It took the jury one hour to come up the the 'Not Guilty' and most of that time was spent eating lunch.

I ended the presentation with a pony story, everybody loves ponies. The A.D.A had a story too, except her story began, "When I was in law school …". When she started out with that they all crossed their arms and legs and sneered. Who wants to hear about law school? We wanna hear about the pony!

Anyway, on the relation to meditation. As I said, I was doing four to five hours meditating prior to trial, and still with it during. When I was picking the jury, during the presentation of the case … I honestly felt as though somehow, there was a connection going on that was way beyond the physical. I mean, I felt as though we were connected on some astral plane that was so ethereal and cosmic, that our minds were linked. I would look right over there in the jury box and make eye contact without any discomfort. I sensed they were on my side and in the end they came through for me. They didn't like being lied to by the prosecution. But I can't help but feel that meditation was the secret ingredient in a not guilty verdict.

Over the years meditation has helped me many, many times. Being in prison you encounter some pretty difficult stuff, without it I doubt I'd have been able to cope as well as I have. I recommend it to everybody.

As for my adventures in court … I had only just begun to tap the mine of the limitlessness that opening the mind with meditation and higher awareness can bring. I'd won a battle but the war was on-going. The same A.D.A. and I would meet again in my main case. This time I had a legit, state-paid attorney fighting for me. Joe Hunt told me before he caught the chain to state prison, "You HAVE to take that one pro-per as well … it's the only chance." I just couldn't do it at that time, though. We got slaughtered. Payback for humiliating my opponent on the previous case.

I still had a very long way to go to reach where I needed to be, apparently. All the way to Corcoran State Prison.

"The soul of the world tests all we've learned – most fail the test, they die of thirst with the oasis in sight."

– from <u>The Alchemist</u>

D. Razor Babb

CHAPTER EIGHT: THE ROOT OF THE EVIL

Crossroads

From where I stand I clearly see
The courses laid that beckon me
To the left the path is true
The meadows lush, the water blue
And to the right, a gnarled old tree
Down the lane it calls to me …
'Come hither, lad, the time is nigh'
And yet I linger, by and by
Haste is waste, and 'fore I tread
I hesitate to leave this bed
Of contemplative, mellow joy
Built of dreams since man was boy
Up to this point it's always been
A troubled path, since way back when
Filled with struggle, sorrow, pain
Wind and storm and clouds and rain
And just when sun has dried the sky
And doves and robins sing and fly
My feet are light, my mind is clear
No linger'n hate or worried fear
I hesitate and pause, before
I cross the gate, go through the door
That leads my life a final time
Toward destiny thine fate of mine
And though that path of blissful light
Hath brought a tear of joy this night
'Tis not my destined fate at all
For toward that gnarled old tree I crawl.
And even as I wonder why, I've chosen wrong again, I cry
A voice I hear so clearly say
'The easy path is not thine way.'
– DRB

Alcoholics Anonymous has been around since the 1930's and it's estimated that over two million people have recovered through their program. It's based on some very sound principles and if you are serious about personal rehabilitation, I'd recommend you check out a meeting if they're available at your institution. You may write for information at:

Alcoholics Anonymous
Box 459
Grand Central Stations
New York, N 10163

Their handbook emphasizes in Step Four that the very instincts that nature gave us for survival may, at times, overcome and dominate our behavior – exceeding their natural, proper functions. Desires for sex, material or emotional security, or ego stroking, can overwhelm us and lead to serious trouble. Almost any noticeable emotional problem can be ascribed to misdirected instinct.

By understanding how and when our instincts have gone, or are going haywire, we can begin to harness and correct our behavior. Problems arise when we put instinctive desires ahead of all other things. For example, if we make sex drive paramount, the urge can destroy any chance at material security or emotional stability and ruin our social standing. Or, if we obsess over financial gain above all other considerations, family, friends and other interactions may suffer. Becoming overly emotionally needy can create problems. Whatever the instinct, if it is imposed unreasonably upon others, trouble ensues.

Greed, anger, jealousy, revenge, lust, pride ... if allowed to run your life, can ruin it. It is these underlying instinctual cravings and desire which, many times, lead us to substance abuse and/or criminal behavior. We engage in dinking and drug use to numb feelings of frustration and depression – or, to escape feelings of guilt from engaging in the excesses of our instinctual passions.

AA points out that the substance abuse is really just a symptom of the greater underlying cause. Even if you quit drinking or doping, the character flaws remain – until you recognize and take hold of them.

One reassuring fact in this mess is – everybody has issues! And that's a very inclusive club because 'everybody' doesn't leave too many out. From the most successful person you know, to the lowest, grimiest cretin in the block, we all have issues. So don't feel so all alone. And, everybody has excuses for bad conduct. Hard times, lack of love or understanding, bad health, extreme difficulty, cloying partners, the weather … all those are outside factors when in reality, it's something INSIDE where everything originates. And it's so easy to see faults in others but so difficult to pinpoint what's wrong with 'self'.

Being critical of others while unseeing of our own foibles leads to unbalanced, unstable relationships. It's one of the main reasons we're unable to form genuine bonds with others. Personal maladies tend to fall into two main categories: Either we become dominating and thereby overbearing to people we know, or, we grow so dependent upon others that we become burdensome.

All the while, our insecurities increase and our behavior worsens. Eventually, it becomes impossible for others to meet our demands and unreasonable expectations and we react by trying to manipulate or blame. This causes others to resist or rebel and avoid contact – creating a heightened sense of persecution (in our maladjusted minds), leading to ill-feelings or even a desire to retaliate. Sound familiar? In places like I'm living, it's more the norm than normal. Yes, I can see it in others before I recognize it in myself, and I'm AWARE of the dynamics.

Without guidance or self-examination these issues may escalate to the point of aberrant behavior, further substance abuse, or even criminality. It is ego-driven, self-centered behavior, and contrary to normal functioning productivity. And, most of the time we don't even know when we're doing it. You can always tell when you're on a right or wrong path by the way you feel. Simply stop and ask yourself, "How do I feel?" If the answer is: angry, upset, bothered, annoyed, condemned, depressed, irksome, or enraged ... that's a pretty good clue that something's out of whack. A normally functioning person, while occasionally encountering difficulties will return to normalcy quickly, after addressing any issue that's bothering them. They would answer the same question with responses that are happy, content, enthused, optimistic, or hopeful.

How you 'feel' is an indicator of what track you're on and where you're headed. And, remember, you attract the same type of energy, thought, person, circumstance or thing you're giving out. You've got to monitor your thoughts and feelings constantly.

If you were heading out on a car trip you would surely check your oil, water, tire pressure, and gas before embarking on the journey. How much more important is your life and psyche? If your engine was overheating wouldn't you stop and add water? If the oil light went on, wouldn't you stop and get oil? Why wouldn't you pay as much heed to your own mentality and personality as you would to your car? The problem is, among many, that we just don't think in these terms normally and the neglect is killing us. What's really shameful is, we're doing it to ourselves.

Love yourself enough, or at least look out for yourself enough to dig down to the root of the problems that seem to recur so often. The results are worth it.

Instinctive behavioral pulls so many times mislead us to our folly. If you are reading this, it means you care about your life and you want to be the kind of person you wouldn't mind meeting, yourself. It's all within your power. It takes commitment, it takes strength of character ... and courage.

"To attain true inner freedom you must be able to objectively observe your problems instead of being lost in them. Once you've made that commitment to free yourself of that scared person inside, you will notice that there is a clear decision point at which your growth will take place."

– from <u>The Untethered Soul</u>
Michael Singer

"When personality comes fully to serve the energy of the soul, that is authentic empowerment."

– from <u>The Seat of the Soul</u>
Gary Zucker

When you transcend ego in favor of a higher form of consciousness, you will join humanity and experience an entirely new way of experiencing the world.

CHAPTER NINE: PREPARING FOR PAROLE

In many cases personal rehabilitation may be followed, or go hand-in-hand, with parole consideration. In that case you will be appearing before a parole board who will want to know whether you are suitable for release. Major evolution in state and federal case law now enables lifers, and those with beyond life terms, to appear before the board with the hope of showing that they are no longer dangerous, and have come to an understanding of what led to their crime(s) and how it hurt the victims (and members of their own family), with complete transparency, and get positive results by exhibiting insight, responsibility and understanding of their conduct.

We have begun to delve into personal insights and moral conduct, in this chapter we will examine how the heightened awareness of self and the interconnectedness of everyone and everything, might be directed toward a positive resulting in the parole hearing.

First, it is important to understand the legal and procedural grounds upon which the board stands. In order to present a thorough case, you have to know the parameters. Case law on the federal level (Biggs, Sass, Irons & Hayward), and on the state level (Lawrence & progeny) has placed the lifer issue on two major factors:

1)	Extensive Drug and Behavior Rehabilitation Therapy, and

2) The Ability to Express Personal Insight

'Insight', for Board and Psych evaluation purposes, means the ability to express:

1) Full personal and moral responsibility for your crimes, regardless of your individual level of participation (including details and facts that may have not been known previously, which you may use to broaden, not minimize, you culpability). Yes, it is advisable to maximize culpability.

2) An understanding of the underlying factors of your antisocial mindset and behavior (childhood or adolescent experiences and how they negatively altered your personal identity and thinking).

3) The impact of such antisocial thinking and behavior on your victims. (You must refer to your victims by name and empathize on an emotional level as to how your crimes caused trauma and impacted their lives, including those indirectly affected – such as victims' family members and unborn children. In cases of murder, these are the children who will never live because of your actions).

Following are five major areas that will be covered in a board hearing or by a psychological examiner:

1) Underlying factors of your criminal behavior:
    a. Childhood experiences or trauma
    b. Shaping influences
2) Facts surrounding the crime itself:
    a. Details
    b. Sequence of events
    c. Who did what, when, how, where and why

3) Post-incarceration:
    a. Therapy you have received
    b. Therapy you help provide for others
4) How you feel about the crime today:
    a. Murder is the worst crime one person can commit against another.
    b. Not only did you kill one person, you killed a piece of everyone who loved that person. In this way, murder is really multiple murder.
5) Parole plans:
    a. Residence arrangement
    b. Job arrangements
    c. Relapse prevention: location of and contact with a 12-step program in your area
    d. Financial support from whomever constitutes your support team

In today's world, "Incontrovertible rehabilitative efforts" and "insight" are the main factors in consideration for release. Legally, far less emphasis can be place on crime factors alone. According to law:

> " ... due consideration of the specified factors requires more than rote recitation of the relevant factors with no reasoning establishing a rational nexus between those factors and the necessary basis for the ultimate decision – the determination of current dangerousness." (See: <u>In re Lawrence,</u> supra at 1210).

"Mere recitation of the circumstances of the commitment offense, absent articulation of a rational nexus between those facts and current dangerousness, fails to provide the require 'modicum of evidence' of suitability. (<u>In re Lawrence</u>, supra at 1227).

'Nexus' means connection. There has to be some logical connection between your case factors or prior criminality on the one hand, and something going on today that indicates 'rationally' that you are a current danger to society. 'Reasoning' calls for a logical explanation by the Board or Governor to deny parole. This is the mandate of California Supreme Court rulings. The mandate is not optional and you need to digest that. In order to present your case correctly you present evidence to erase any indication that there is a nexus or connection that you are still dangerous, you must make it obvious that the Board or Governor cannot find 'rational nexus' to your dangerousness, your <u>current dangerousness,</u> because there isn't any!

It is your mission and your challenge to make it impossible to show that you are still a danger, you understand your criminal behavior, and you have made steps to rehabilitate yourself.

<u>'Lack of Insight'</u> is being used to deny parole, you must understand this concept backwards and forwards. The California Supreme Court, in defining and dissecting what constitutes "some evidence" in parole cases, as it relates to "current dangerousness" has given the board and governor some wiggle room. In denying parole the BPH and Governor are using the following:

> "In some cases, such as those in which the inmate has failed to make efforts toward rehabilitation, has continued to engage in criminal conduct post-incarceration, or has shown a lack of insight or remorse,

the aggravated circumstances of the commitment offense may well continue to prove 'some evidence' of current dangerousness even decades after omission of the offense." (In re Lawrence, supra at 1228).

You have to understand the law and how it is being used in the context of the BPH in order to be able to jump the hurdles even before they're in place. The approach to the BPH must conform to the law and spirit of the time. According to current law and the atmosphere of review criteria it's necessary for a prisoner to 'come clean' on all issues. Why wouldn't you? You've already been convicted, you've already done the time, now you're up for parole and it's time to go home.

At the hearing you must present a candid, revealing picture of your previous lifestyle, how you became involved in it, and even convey information that was previously unknown – explain how bad your life really was, how you let your family down, how you squandered opportunities and how you could have exercised other options. Admit your foolishness and twisted thinking and how it affected other's lives.

In a previous chapter we discussed how you must make a personal inventory of wrongs committed and understand the nature of your wrong behavior. This is the time to reveal that to the board. It's covered well in the AA program in steps #4 and #5. Get the AA handbook and delve into it. Understand and claim full responsibility for your actions and the results of your acts. The gangs or drugs or other manifestations and methods of your actions are only vehicles of wrong-doing. The real motivation is underlying in your personality disorder(s). Come to grips with that, admit it.

Be forthcoming in your presentation as to your understanding that it was your own foolishness which led you to where you are today. You knew the consequences of drug use and gang involvement before you undertook the path which led to wrong acts. Be very clear on this.

Your previous mindset and lifestyle, however awful it may have been, must make sense to you before you can explain it in terms that are logical to others. You have to come to terms in your own mind as to how you got in a gang, how you got involved in drugs, how you came to your criminal behavior.

Ask yourself, "What actually happened to my life? What happened to me? How did this happen, where did I go wrong?" Then, explain it to yourself. It has to make sense (to you) so you can relay it to the board. Holes or gaps in any story will be interpreted as either being lies, or showing a lack of understanding of self. You can't afford that perception. They won't trust you or your story if it doesn't make sense. Encourage the board to ask questions, the questions they ask are the areas in which you were unclear.

Don't avoid the tough issues, face them and deal with them squarely. The board needs a complete and plausible story from you or else they don't have a valid reason to help you parole. They wouldn't be able to defend your parole suitability or judicial relief without you providing the testimonial evidence. You are narrating the story of your life, you're presenting that story to this group of strangers in order for them to 'get it' and to see and realize, logically, how you got here. And, how you now understand where and why you went wrong. You have to be completely open, candid and forthright. Lay your cards on the table shamelessly, this is your chance to put it all out there. There is absolutely no reason to hold back now. Compose your story, write it out, make notes that you can refer to when telling the board, practice reciting the story out loud and even memorize it.

This has to be done.

Make an outline to refer to for your presentation. You have to insure you get everything pertinent into the transcript of the hearing – in case of a denial, relief may be possible in the courts. Every bit of information you need in order to obtain your freedom must be on the transcript record.

A panel or judge must be able to justify your suitability or relief, to their own bosses. You must give them every opportunity to do so. Commissioners and judges have to answer to somebody. When a commissioner or judge is on your side, you'll find they will make your case better than you did. This is because they have to justify their decisions to supervisors, who, understandably, tend to have a higher legal and professional standard of review. No one wants his or her decision overturned, nor does anyone want to be perceived as soft-on-crime, supporting or releasing life-prisoners unjustifiably. Remember, there is a human and political factor at play, as well. People must be able to make sense of your entire life's scenario, and come to the conclusion that, under the law, you have something good coming at this point. But, only you can give them the narrative that gives them a complete picture. This level of personal exposure will not make your commitment offenses any less disturbing, but it will make it more understandable.

If they understand you, if your story makes perfect sense, it's much easier for them to support a favorable review and see you as a likely candidate for release.

Next area of importance, cleaning up the record. By law, the BPH must give you the opportunity to correct and clarify the record. You simply state, "I would like to correct and/or clarify the record." They must stop and listen. Review all documents, transcripts and information available to you checking for mistakes, inaccuracies and discrepancies in all documents and between all documents. This includes the Investigative Crime Report (original police report). Know what co-defendants said, know what confidential information assertions were made, and the D.A.'s parole opposition info. Take note of specific documents and page numbers where there are mistakes, inaccuracies or discrepancies. And clear up the record accordingly.

In previous transcripts, look for opportunities to provide a more clear or complete picture of the scenario surrounding your commitment offense. If you misspoke in previous hearings, correct and clarify the record in the hearing. In your preparation, go through all previous transcripts and answer every question you were ever asked, again (to yourself). What are issues of confusion or contention? You may want to use the 'correct and clarify' opportunity to re-answer past questions. Straighten everything out, point by point, expanding on issues that were previously a problem. Refer, on the record, to specific documents, forms, reports or transcripts (date, page, line). If your story has changed, or it seems as though it has, clarify the reasons why that is so. Be concise, but leave nothing out.

Next up, undermining the arguments against your parole. What are the strengths in the argument opposing your parole? Put yourself in the shoes of those who wouldn't want you out. Identify with the opposition and see it from their viewpoint. What is their strongest point? What is the overall basis of the opposition? How will they frame arguments? And, where are you vulnerable? Don't soft-sell this or hide from painful or embarrassing facts. Emphasize and maximize the issues against you so you'll be prepared for the onslaught of negativity that WILL come.

You are in the best position to articulate the insightful moral outrage that needs to be displayed. You neutralize the opponent's case against you by bringing up the tough stuff yourself, and emphasizing it harsher than even they would! Only you know what a despicable character you were at the time, and you can vocalize that and demonstrate it better than anyone. If you don't, they will. Don't go light. Go hard. Then, all the good rehab and introspection you have done will have true validity. By painting this horrible picture of yourself, by the time the opposition gets to it, all the shock value is gone and it will seem like nothing more than piling on.

The ADA speaks their opposition piece toward the end of the hearing. You have to assert yourself first, showing that you understand the terrible nature of your actions, before they speak. This shows that you've come to terms with who you were and how awful and destructive your life was. Believe me, somebody is going to try and make you look like the embodiment of evil, it might as well be you. You've made the moral inventory already, share it with the board. Nobody can do it better.

Next: <u>The packet.</u> Your Lifer Board Packet is a thick folder compiling all the documented material related to you and your offense. It's a very important article as it relates to your suitability for parole. You must be in possession of this artifact. Every person in the room is operating from the perspective of this documentation. If you choose to represent yourself at the hearing, your Lifer Board Packet will be presented to you, otherwise the BPH-appointed attorney will receive it, and you may never see it.

If you intend to be represented by counsel, even a BPH-appointed one, when you meet him find out what you have to do in order to get a copy of your packet. Get your family involved, offer to pay for it, document his response. He's only getting a token payment for his services, and the state's paying him, so don't rely on him for much. He won't review your packet very well, he doesn't have time. You are not special to an appointed attorney. No one is going to represent you like you will, you are your best advocate.

And, with your packet in your own possession, you'll have details and information to work with.

<u>The transcript.</u> The record that emerges from your board hearing may be the most important article you'll ever have. When you speak into that microphone you are laying evidence for your release. You want everything you say 'on the record'. The transcript is the vital legal document that must be filed in court if you get a denial unjustifiably. It's legal ground is:

<u>IN LIGHT OF COMMITMENT OFFENSES (PRISTINE POST-CONVICTION RECORD), EXTENSIVE REHABILITATION AND REQUISITE INSIGHT, THE PAROLE BOARD (OR GOVERNOR) ARTICULATED NO NEXUS-EVIDENCE THAT IMPLIES, PORTENDS, OR RATIONALLY INDICATES PETITIONER IS A CURRENT OR FUTURE UNREASONABLE RISK OF DANGER TO</u>

PUBLIC SAFTEY: THEREFORE, THERE IS NO LEGAL BASIS UPON WHICH TO DENY PAROLE AT THIS TIME.

It is on the BPH Panel/Governor to rationally articulate through demonstrable evidence on the record why you are an unreasonable risk of danger to the public safety.

The California Court of Appeals made it plain in a case favorable to the lifer:

> "The Board/Governor's decision is flawed because it does not contain an explicit articulation of a rational nexus ... and it would be inappropriate for the courts to salvage the Board/Governor's inadequate findings not articulated in the parole decision." In re Timothy Ellis Ross (2009) C.A. 4th, DJDAR 1944, 1951, citing In re Lawrence at 1227 and In re Roderick (2007) 154 C.A. 4th 242, 265.

> "Even where a finding is supported by some evidence a court may determine that the evidence has no connection to the inmate's potential dangerousness.... In some cases ... the evidence may be so disassociated from the paramount concern that it cannot, as a matter of law, support a decision denying parole. In that situation, it is incumbent upon the court to insure that the Board/Governor's decision does not turn upon such evidence." In re Criscione, (2009) C.A. 4th, DJDAR

5448, 5452.

"The relevant inquiry is whether the circumstances of the commitment offense, when considered in light of the other facts in the record, are such that they continue to be predictive of current dangerousness." In re Lawrence @1221.

It is true that an extensive period of clean-time and education/vocational achievement are important, but 'extensive drug and behavior rehabilitation therapy' and 'insight' are the bull's eye of the target. To be precise, 'extensive drug and behavior rehab therapy and insight' are so important, that the Lifer's Board and Litigation Preparation Guide, from which this chapter is gleaned, says, "YOU NAIL THIS AND YOU WALK!"

Now, keep in mind, the opposition is working with the same target, and their aim is to make you miss or undermine your attempt. Once you correct and clarify the record of all mistakes, inaccuracies and discrepancies, and present a clear and graphic picture of what happened to your life, it's all about what you've done to address your personal issues since your incarceration began. You must also be prepared to express in detail the personal revelations you have had as a result of your rehabilitative therapy and your personal insight regarding the underlying factors of your criminal behavior, the crime itself, and how you feel about it today. You want all of this on the record and you want it highlighted in your presentation.

You have to take the initiative, don't wait for the right time or to be asked, it is up to you to seize the moment. It won't take them long to realize that you know exactly what you're doing, everybody knows the 'insight' game, it's no secret. That's why you have to be 'real', and authentic. The previous chapters of this book emphasized how to be that type of person. If you're not there yet, go back and review. Find that core depth inside that makes you human and connect to your humanity. If you're real, it will come through. If you're not, it'll show worse than a bad hair piece.

The point you are making in your presentation is that you now fully understand what happened, how it happened, and as a result, you have taken extensive measures to ensure it can never happen again. In fact, you want to help prevent it from happening to others who are just like you. You have to accept full and complete responsibility for your commitment offense, and full moral culpability for the harm your actions have perpetuated afterwards. And as a result, you have become a completely different person than you were at the time of the offense. You have accomplished this through the insight you've gained through extensive drug and rehabilitation therapy over multiple years Evidence of your insight and incontrovertible rehabilitative efforts must be on the record, not only with documentary evidence (chronos and certificates, etc.) but with verbal evidence. The upshot of your entire presentation is that there is no way you can possibly be "an unreasonable risk of danger to the public" at this point. In fact, the record is replete with information indicating that you would actually be an extraordinary asset to society now. This is why your Board presentation must be filled with evidence of articulated "Insight" and rehabilitation therapy, which must overshadow all else. You need every chrono and certificate available to you – multiple times over, in successive years. Every chrono and certificate you obtain is one more brick in the narrative you are building for your freedom.

At the end of the hearing you must be able to stand firmly on "profound and thorough insight" and "extensive drug and behavior therapy", the twin pillars of the present-day freedom archway. You must be able to declare definitively and convincingly in your closing argument: "I am clearly no longer an unreasonable risk of danger to public safety, and there is absolutely no evidence to the contrary. In fact, at this point in my life and development, the record is replete with evidence that I would be an extraordinary asset to my community." Force the Board or Governor to demonstrate how your profound and thorough insight combined with your extensive rehabilitation does not completely nullify the type of person you were at the time of the commitment offense. This is why you must, with precision, express exactly how every aspect of your dysfunctional lifestyle has been specifically addressed. Be prepared always to say, "I have excellent insight on this or that issue, and I would like to elaborate." You must know every step of the 12-step program of AA/NA and be prepared to discuss them at the drop of a dime, even if your crimes had nothing to do with drugs or alcohol. Criminal behavior can be as addicting as any drug. You need to be able to articulate the 12-step principles as a sign that you understand this.

AA/NA goes beyond alcohol and drug issues. They address the underlying factors which led to the substance abuse – therein lies the real personality problems which led us here. You must be aware of these issues, otherwise, you're not ready to be released.

Be able to verbalize exactly when your mental rehabilitative transition took place. It's called 'the tipping point'. Talk about some event that caused your mind to change, some revelation or epiphany you may have experienced that was the 'tipping point' in your rehabilitative transition.

Leave no stone unturned, no bell un-rung. Be willing and able to discuss each and every program in which you participated, and how you grew from it. Give the opposition no 'wiggle room' whatsoever. If there are closed-circuit institutional TV therapeutic programs at your institution, many times these are a great source of rehabilitative therapy and many times offer chronos or certificates. Take full advantage. The nature of this fight is your "insight derived from your extensive drug and behavior rehabilitation therapy" versus your "previous antisocial mindset and behavior." The law is structured to determine whether you remain an "unreasonable risk of danger to public safety."

Both victory and defeat are within your grasp. You must make sure that your "insight derived from our extensive drug and behavior rehabilitation therapy" completely addresses, subdues, and obliterates you "previous antisocial mindset and behavior", and is articulated on the record. The BPH Panel's presence simply affords you the opportunity to get on the microphone. What you say into that boardroom microphone is going to make you or break you! The transcript you create in the boardroom is your 'insurance policy'. This is the only thing that will stand up in court and secure your freedom.

<u>Create your own Board portfolio.</u> Obtain an easily-accessible two-hole punch press-board folder. Use manila file-folders to separate it into sections. The will be the equivalent of your own personal mini C-File. The difference, of course, is that you control what it contains. Your Board portfolio will speak volumes about you. The fact that you have gone to the trouble of creating one says something about you. Your CDCR Central File is rather large, bulky, and cumbersome. It contains every shred of written information ever generated about you since your incarceration

began. No one really wants to go through all that stuff to find something good about you. Your personal Board portfolio gives the Panel an alternate source of information.

Your personal portfolio must be a neat, orderly and compact compilation of all your achievements, in chronological order. Make it appealing to the eye, presentation is everything. Inside the front cover list a table of contents with a chronological list of all the chronos, certificates, college course report cards, letters from correspondences for moral, housing and employment support, community-based 12-step programs, relapse prevention plans, even family photos. A few selected photos may humanize you. The fact is, you are a part of a family – you weren't always the evil, no-good, low down, mangy character that came to the joint.

Your chronos should be taped top to bottom in an overlapping format. If you have lost or misplaced any chrono or certificate, document them in your chronological list anyway. You have a right to an Olsen Review of your Central File. Go to the chrono/certificate section and write down anything you may be missing. List every positive chrono and certificate issued to you, including job performance chronos. Sometimes the originals don't find their way into your C-File, everything positive about you must be in your personal portfolio.

Take control. You must not depend upon an attorney to secure your freedom. If you can read, write and effectively speak for yourself, if there is an attorney present, especially a BPH-appointed one, he should be a mere formality. You must not put yourself in a position of dependency. You have to be in charge. An attorney is only necessary for those who are afraid to speak or not mentally or physically able to. You are not a real client to a

BPH-appointed attorney. You are just another lifer-inmate, another number among many. He doesn't have time for you, or the energy to go through your Lifer Packet looking for details that will help you. Someone needs to do that, and that someone is YOU. And he can actually be a liability!

The fewer people in the room, the better. The Board wants and needs to hear from YOU. An attorney can actually be a distraction and get in the way. The Panel probably knows whoever it is that's representing you, they've probably heard his spiel before, many times. They already have an opinion of him. They might even be tired of listening to his voice from all his previous representations. You are the most qualified person there is to speak about yourself. This is about your life – get in there and take control of the situation. Everyone is there to determine what's going to happen with your life, shouldn't you be the one making the case for a positive result?

If you feel you HAVE to have an attorney there, then at least insist on full cooperation from him. He works for you. First, you need a copy of your Lifer Board Packet, several weeks before your hearing. Offer to pay for it, do whatever it takes. There are obscure but vital details about you in there, and your victims, like, their names, ages, siblings. These are real people with real lives and you messed them up. How can you reveal true insight when you haven't even personalized your victims?

You need to prepare for everything that can possibly be used against you. There's nothing worse than being blind-sided in the boardroom. There are valuable jewels buried in your Lifer Board Packet. As soon as the ADA detects that you have not studied your Packet, he will twist your entire presentation. He will be able to imply and assert anything he wants – and he will! At best, all you'll be able to do is deny it. But you won't have anything concrete upon which to stand. The ADA is a pro at making unprepared witnesses look terrible, even when they're telling the truth. They went to law school!

This is what they do for a living! An experienced lawyer can shred a witness without ANY preparation. That's because they use the same technique on any and all witnesses and they've done this same song and dance over and over. They're going to interrupt, come at you aggressively, their tone of voice will imply that you're lying or don't know what you're talking about. They'll try to upset you, antagonize you or throw you off you game in any way necessary in order to gain control of the interaction. It's a game to them. Honestly, it's no skin off their noses if you get out or stay in. They probably even know that you're an okay guy, now, and will do fine outside. But ... lawyers are ego-driven. They want to win. This is why they're lawyers!

Man, you're heading into the cage with a shark and you better be prepared. If you were going into a physical battle, you'd be prepared. If you were heading into a sporting competition you'd practice up. Even if you were going to a card or chess tournament, you'd practice, prepare and be ready. This is beyond all that! You have to be ready. Get your Packet, get in there and dig. If you're better prepared than the other guy, guess who has the advantage? No one should know your Packet better than you do. If your lawyer wants to help you, he'll get you a copy of your Packet. As a last resort you can ask him to look over his copy for a couple of weeks. It's better than nothing.

Cite document, page, paragraph and the Board will take notice. You are the best person alive to weave together a cohesive case for parole. There is too much at stake to sit there and 'let' it happen. Step up it's your turn to bat. You have to swing for the fences!

<u>Your support letters.</u> Get your support letters together. Solid parole plans are important. The most effective method is to have one responsible family member coordinate your contacts. If one family member can manage the collection of letters and mail them all to you at once it is more convenient for you. All letters concerning living arrangements and work opportunities must be no more than one year old. Postponements occur in hearings, have your letters dated accordingly. Living arrangements and job offers must be separate letters. Employment offers should be on letterhead and be specific concerning what the job offer is. The more precise, the better. Once they arrive get your counselor to make copies with the original to place in your file. You can't trust they'll find their way in, though, so have copies for your portfolio. If letters arrive too late for a Central-File placement, bring them into the hearing anyway. You have that right, by law.

Make contact with a substance-abuse agency in the area in which you are paroling, a place where you can attend AA/NA 12-step meetings. You need a letter or at least a pamphlet or some form of documentation indicating the locations and days and times of meeting. This information should be dated within the one-year time frame.

<u>115's and 128's.</u> Recent 115's and 128's aren't good for anyone, especially for anyone going to Board. There should be a significant distance of years, the more the better, between your last 115 and your hearing.

There, of course, is a significant difference between willful rules violations and honest misunderstandings. Petty 115's and 128's generally can be explained away as legit mistakes or misunderstandings. You must do the explaining.

You are in an environment where, technically, honest mistakes and misunderstandings can be documented and punished as severely as willful violations of rules and regulations – and many times are. This is the nature of the prison environment And, according to law, honest mistakes and misunderstandings, just like any other factor, establishes:

> "... unsuitability if, and only if, those circumstance are probative to the determination that a prisoner remains a danger to the public." In re Lawrence, supra @ 1212.

Just because you have encountered an honest mistake or misunderstanding and it was documented, doesn't necessarily mean you are "an unreasonable risk of danger to public safety" any more than a parking ticket indicates that a car owner is unfit for society. Don't be overly intimidated by the issue. Meet it head on. Bring it up. Your plausible explanation will be in the transcript. Stress the fact that your mistakes and misunderstandings were honest. Everyone makes mistakes, including BPH members. No one is immune, so be up front and bring the issue up first so you are the one framing the discussion.

If you have willful 115s that reach back before your "extensive drug and rehabilitation therapy" come clean in the same way that you were regarding your previous lifestyle. These violations must be explained as a continuation of that prior mindset, in which you no longer partake. This enables you to more dramatically illustrate your "clean break" with the past after you began your "extensive drug and behavior rehabilitation therapy".

There needs to be a time in your incarceration where there was an obvious and dramatic change in you and your behavior. You need to be able to present evidence of that sea change. The tipping point, the significant milestone, the event, circumstance or epiphany that suddenly opened your eyes and a new day dawned. There comes a time when every lifer who is serious about freedom, must cease all willful violations of rules and regulations. They can cost you many years. Younger lifers should be particularly aware of this. Many of the other guys you hang with already have dates and will be long gone when you're still doing time for acts you may have felt compelled to do. At this time, the doors are open ... but, that could change.

<u>Your psych evaluation.</u> You must approach your psychological evaluation just as you approach the Board. Come clean, ring the bell first, present your portfolio. The same principles apply with the psych evaluator as applies to your presentation to the Board. Even if you are not admitting guilt of the crime, be prepared to articulate insight as it relates to what the victims have gone through and the impact the crime has had on them. Be able to empathize on the emotional level of a citizen, even if you insist you had nothing to do with the crime. Make it impossible for the Psych professional to conclude that you are a "high risk for recidivism" and you "lack insight".

You might want to consider hiring a private Psychologist if possible. The appointed Psyche is only interested in assessing insight as it pertains to your admission of guilt, even though the law says you don't have to admit guilt. Whoever interviews you, you have to show regret and remorse. They are similar, but remorse is indicative of penitence. Know the difference.

An important note on the Psyche evaluation interview. Get your support letters in early enough so you have them for this. It relates to the Psyche's evaluation of your family support and parole plans.

CONCLUSION

Proper preparation and information is the key to a Board hearing. There has been groundbreaking litigation done in recent years and the judicial landscape has been dramatically altered. It's important to know, more lifers go home through the courts than do through the Board. You set your foundation for court in what you plant in the record. Don't hold back.

I've done over 22 years on a beyond life sentence. Without an 'L', even with halftime it has always seemed impossible and improbable that I'd ever go home. All this time there hasn't been an avenue for review of someone without an 'L', except clemency review. A year ago they instituted the 25/60 rule. Twenty-five years in and sixty years of age up, you get a hearing. That's three years off for me.

Eleven days ago, out of the blue, they advised me I have a Board hearing in sixty days. That might have been a result of the clemency petition I filed a year ago, or maybe there are bigger forces at work. I don't think many first timers to the BPH go home, the statistics must be astoundingly against that. But, I've faced long odds before. Wayne Dyer wrote in <u>Power of Intention</u>, "Stay tuned vibrationally to the Source of all life and all the power of that field of intention that intended you and everyone else here will cooperate to bring into your life what you desire." That's a valuable, and I'm hoping, prophetic teaching.

CHAPTER TEN: INSIGHT

Whether you are preparing for a Board hearing or trying to straighten your life out for more personal reasons, insight into your prior behavior is the key to unlocking not only the jailhouse door, but the vast and mysterious portal of your mind. By understanding 'self', we may begin to journey beyond the limitations of what we thought was possible before. But first, we must gain insight.

Insight – 1. The ability to see and understand clearly the inner nature of things, esp. by intuition. 2. A clear understanding of the inner nature of some specific thing. 3. a) Psychological awareness of one's own mental attitude and behavior; b) In Psychiatry, a recognition of one's own mental disorder.

With the Webster's Dictionary definition, we begin to realize why such importance is bestowed upon the word, 'insight'. Here, we will cover insight as it pertains to a parole board hearing as outlined in the summer, 2009 article of *Parole Matters*.

Insight is being used not only as an integral part of a prisoner's potential FOR release ... but also as a major reason given for DENYING parole. This is because it can act as the connection between your criminal behavior and a present risk to public safety. As you may well know, the courts agree that a historical factor like your present crime or your priors cannot be used to deny parole unless there is a nexus between these factors and a present risk to public safety. Therefore, the easiest thing for the Board to rely on is 'insight' because: a) it is an inherently subjective thing to prove and it leaves the Board with the opportunity to pick apart your presentation without citing specific facts; b) many inmates fail to explicitly detail their insight into the crime; c) the pivotal California Supreme Court case <u>In re Shaputis</u> allows the Board to deny parole solely because of the lack of insight; and d) many inmates actually lack insight.

Thus, insight is the simplest way to deny parole when no other reason exists.

Insight has three major parts: 1) Agreement with the court's version of the crime. 2) Understanding into what makes your crime different from others. 3) Insight into your remorse, acceptance of responsibility and understanding of WHY the crime occurred.

INSIGHT INTO WHAT? The most tested area of insight focused on by the Board is insight into your crime. But, insight can also apply to your priors and your social history. For Board purposes, insight into your crime is paramount and a thorough understanding of this essential.

INSIGHT ABOUT WHAT? About your crime, yes, but what specifically? Generally, you need an understanding of three main factors: 1) Facts, 2) Defining characteristics of your crime, and 3) Remorse.

    1)   <u>Get the facts right.</u> The first and most obvious area of insight relates to your understanding of the basic facts of your case. The

Board wants to see that your understanding corresponds with the court's version. Here, the court's version includes the facts as stated in the Probation Officer's report, as well as any Court of Appeals decision, among other sources. The Board wants to confirm that your understanding of the facts doesn't contradict what the court believed happened. For most inmates, this is not a problem unless you are of the belief you are innocent of the crime. For the innocent, this part of insight can be difficult to deal with. For those guilty of their crimes, it boils down to agreeing with the court's version and remembering (to the best of your ability) exactly what occurred. For example, the Board can determine lack of insight when an inmate cannot recall essential facts of the crime that he should know despite (perhaps) being intoxicated during the commission of the crime. Here, it is crucial to agree with the court's version and be able to recall the facts in as much detail as possible.

The board is basically testing your honesty and acceptance of responsibility. If you are forgetting key facts they may conclude you are doing so deliberately as a way to minimize your involvement or culpability, remembering the crime in a way that makes you less accountable. It is best to agree with as much of the court's version as you can and to recall as much of the crime as you can. That's insight.

2) <u>Defining characteristics of your crime.</u> Defining qualities or characteristics means what stands out about your crime that differentiates it from others. This can be a number of things: The extent of your extreme intoxication; the manner of death (in a murder case); the severe extent of injuries; the triviality of the motivation, or depth of reason; your youthful age; the number of victims; the extent

of your attempt to cover or flee from the crime. What stands out that gives your offense its defining qualities? This is especially useful in heinous crimes because when done with complete candor it takes the wind out the sails of any argument put forth by the ADA concerning cruelty, because you're showing insight.

3)   <u>Remorse</u> – a deep, torturing sense of guilt felt over a wrong that one has done; self-reproach. Pity or compassion (for your victim).

Insight into remorse means detailing how you are remorseful and regretful over what you did. Most inmates miss the mark about this critical stage, because they simply state: "I accept full responsibility for my crime." And leave it at that. The means nothing to the Board. They want details, want to know what it is you are accepting responsibility for, and they want to know how you 'feel' about what you've done.

Try this: Imagine the worst thing you've ever done to someone you care about. Actually think back to that moment when you did something that is so disturbing to you that you feel you can never erase the guilt or embarrassment of that act. I know you have these memories, because I have them. They're not necessarily related to your crime, or 'A' crime, but in your heart and mind the event was criminal and you wish you could erase it or do it all over again. Now think back on your crime. Apply the same empathy with your victim(s) as you do with the loved one you mistreated. This is the level of regret and remorse the Board is looking for. This is the degree of remorse you should be striving to achieve in any instance when you've harmed another.

Remember, at our core we are souls inhabiting bodies ... all of our souls are interconnected, ethereal energy, infinite mind matter and all of the same source energy. You can't hurt another without hurting yourself. Now, what do you regret most about your crime? It is helpful to review the events of the day of the incident – that's what the Board is going to want you to do.

On the day of the crime, moment by moment, what were you doing and thinking? What is the biggest regret of that day? How were you living at the time? What could you have done differently? You can discuss how you have dealt with the shame of committing your crime and injuring your victims, as well as expressing remorse by seeing the events through the eyes of the victim, perhaps telling the story of the crime from their standpoint (prior to the hearing). This may reveal a new perspective into what you have done and the harm caused, which can be shared with the Board.

Why did the crime occur? A major area of concern and enlightenment comes when you consider the causative factors that led to the commission of the offense. Reasons can be varied and cumulative, and may include:

- Bad choices
- Normalizing criminal behavior through previous encounters with the law and committing lesser crimes
- Anger and impulse control issues
- Intoxication and drug abuse
- Low self-esteem and depression

- Poor associations

- Lack of coping skills

- Emotional or psychological instability or immaturity

- Stress factors

These are just a few of the many reasons crimes can occur. Your job is to be able to list and detail the reasons that apply to your situation, and show how this led to your criminal act(s). Simply naming the reasons isn't enough – you must show an understanding of the correlation between behavior, impetus and crime.

<u>Responsibility.</u> You must be able to vocalize exactly WHAT you feel you are responsible for. Detail is important. You may be asked to replay the events of your crime and elaborate at what points during its commission you're taking personal responsibility for. This includes being able to accept responsibility for a crime partner's actions, maybe even something the victim did. Once you set into motion a chain of events, you have to own those events and acknowledge that the effects of those decisions, events, results – all stem from your action.

<u>Magnitude and impact.</u> You ultimately have to share insight concerning your crime as it relates to your understanding of the effects and impact it has had on not only the victim, not only yourself ... but the victim's family, the community, witnesses, your family, and others. Do you even know the names of your victims? Have you thought about the immediate and long term effects of your actions on them and others? In the case of murder, it is almost incalculable to assess the damage done because when a life is taken it affects people you not only have

never met, but there are children who might never be born because of you.

Each person's life that we touch is affected by our presence, whether good or bad. Insight means that you can comprehend this concept and can vocalize your understanding of the most difficult and painful aspects of how your conduct has affected others. You can't convey something that isn't there. The first eight chapters of this book show you how to find your humanity and become the kind of person who cares how they impact others. If you can become that type of person, if you ARE that type of person, you can genuinely communicate that to others.

Insight is not an exact science. It comes when you are real about the details you share with the Board in reviewing your life and your crime. It comes when you know what you want to express on these topics before you walk into the room. Insight equally applies to priors and their impact, as well as your responsibility in regards to them, and an understanding of how the events of your life have led you to where you are, and how you intend to stay on a right course from here on out.

Insight requires that you know the moments in your life when you realized things were going wrong; and now you understand cause and effect, and maybe have figured out how to avoid the same mistakes you couldn't avoid before. The kind of mistakes that fill you with regret and remorse and when you think back on them even now give you a sick, queasy feeling in your gut ... a hollowness that eats at you from inside out and you feel like you're going to throw up because you hate who you were and what you did, and you remember the first time you ever felt that way.

For me, it was back in L.A. County in the visiting room. My wife had hauled my eight-year old daughter and one-year old son to the jail to visit me, behind glass. My daughter was stoic, she didn't know how to act, the baby was reaching for me and pounding his fat little hand on the glass. I'm not usually one for sentimentality, but that scene right there ... my heart was being ripped out and there wasn't a single thing I could do about it. That was the moment I knew I'd lost everything that mattered. I never saw my wife and kids after that day. It was for all of their benefit that that was the way it was going to have to be. Even now, 22 plus years later, I still feel the cold sweat of panic and insanity rise up inside. And I know who's to blame.

D. Razor Babb

CHAPTER ELEVEN: WHERE THE WOODS WON'T END

When I began writing this it was meant to be a very basic winnowing down of the most poignant principles and teaching I've encountered over the years, a way to give back and help others so they didn't have to wade through the cluttered bookshelves of self-help, psychology, spirituality and philosophy in order to find the gems that can spur us all to betterment. I thought I'd pepper the chapters with minor vignettes of my own experiences and those of others to add a little spice and break up the monotony of lengthy narrative. But, the thing about writing is, sometimes you have to let it flow through you in order to capture the real stuff. If a baring of soul is required, oh well, it's my duty and responsibility to speak the truth, otherwise, what's the use? We could read and write <u>Twilight</u> and make millions with the mindless drivel. Seriously? Three or four <u>Twilights</u> on the *NY Times* bestseller list at the same time? No wonder it's so obvious the world's coming to an end. Our only hope is that when Trump becomes president he'll fix all that. Back to the real.

When I was a kid in northern Missouri and my psycho stepdad was busy at work all day, and thus unable to vent his psychological and physical abuse in my direction for those few hours, my dog, Kokomo, and I would go explore the woods near our home. We lived a couple of miles outside of town and there weren't any other kids around, so my brown boxer was my only friend and constant companion for most of the years between age four and thirteen.

The woods began about a half mile from the house and extended westward to the old Grand River. During the summer the Grand trickled down to a muddy creek, but when the rains came it overflowed for miles in all directions. The woods ran north and south along the twisting river. Each time we went out we'd go a little farther, we had to gauge distance and time so we could get back home in time to do chores and be there before my stepdad arrived. Control is key to that type of personality.

Reading about Tom Sawyer and Huck Finn in elementary school, it was always my hope we'd find a passage in the woods that would go on and on, a never ending expanse of wild wilderness where endless adventure might be found and lay in wait for the wide-eyed dreamer. With a home life like mine, I hoped there was something better and greater out there … there had to be.

Summer after summer we searched, on the weekends during fall and winter we trekked … looking for that vast wilderness where the woods won't end.

Each time, no matter how fast and far we traveled, the forest always came to an end somewhere, abutting a farmer's plowed field, divided into fenced lots for clover, hay or livestock. A road carved through the pristine foliage for man to tread with wheel and iron. One time I even attempted to build a raft in order to float down the Grand. But it broke apart and Kokomo abandoned ship in disgust at my poor craftsmanship.

Once we came upon a fenced-in pasture with a beautiful white horse corralled there. Someone's well-taken care of pet, no doubt, as it approached us with confident ease. I lured it to the fence and climbed aboard, grabbed the coarse white mane and galloped across the pasture. But fenced pastures have an end, while little boy's dreams do not. We moved on. Another time, Kokomo was leading the way and ran across the path of a wild boar! The thing stood at least four feet tall and outweighed my little dog five times over. Kokomo stood his ground between the wild beast and me, snarling and growling with a ferocity I wasn't aware he possessed. The monster growled back, tusks gleaming and dripping foamy goop from its elongated snout, the hair on Kokomo's back was raised in a strip down his spine and he lowered his head barking and snarling his evilest intent.

I was hollering, "Kokomo! Come here! Get over here! Kokomo!"

He wasn't having it, he wasn't backing down and it was going to be a battle to the death. He was protecting me, standing up against a Goliath who was easily his better, but I don't think he understood that and even if he did, it wouldn't have changed anything.

I didn't know what to do so I just kept yelling. Finally, Kokomo turned his head to see what the hell I was yelling about, and the savage beast took the opportunity to turn on his heels and skedaddle off across the field. Kokomo may have been brave, but he wasn't stupid. He let the varmint go. Only then did he turn back and come to me, head bobbing in humble pride, tail wagging so hard I thought he'd knock a hip out of joint. He was sniffin' and slobberin' and sure enough glad that the whole episode ended without a fight, I'm sure. After that, I knew for certain who my best friend for life was. When they shipped me off at thirteen that was my one regret, leaving Kokomo like that.

I always wondered for how many days, weeks, months he waited expectantly as the school bus drove by on the road, waiting for it to stop and let me off. How long until he gave up hope?

Thirty or so years later, when I was in Highpower on the pro-per side something happened that is so unexplainable it's difficult to relay with the proper gravitas it deserves. There was a guy down from death row, going to court trying to get the noose off his neck. He wasn't what you would call a real stickler for hygiene and his cell was a real snake pit of filth. The guy had a yellowish cast to his complexion and a really bad cough. It wasn't long until the whole tier was infected and coughing, and soon thereafter the bad news came – it was T.B.

Tuberculosis. A lung infection that is super nasty, difficult to deal with and hard to get over. We were on that Highpower single-man cell row, so we were basically on our own to deal with it the best we could. They brought around pills, but it takes weeks and months to recover. My lungs were so full of phlegm that they felt like they weighted an extra twenty pounds each. All you could do was try and cough that stuff up and hope the medication worked.

One night I had fallen into a fitful slumber and was dreaming I was back in Missouri down by the Grand River. I'd tread out in the deeper water and it was beginning to rise about my head. Kokomo was back on the shore, looking in my direction. As the water got deeper, now over my head, I could see the light above, I was being pulled under and couldn't get myself up or out. Kokomo was standing above me, barking incessantly. I mean just bark, bark, barking, he wouldn't stop. All I wanted to do was fall into a deeper sleep, it was peaceful under the water, quiet and everything was safe and warm there, except for Kokomo's damn barking! He wouldn't let me sleep!

I mean it was one of those barking fits where you're just so annoyed you want to shake him and tell him to shut up! And there he was, standing over me, his image distorted by the water, and he would not let me sleep! Bark, bark, BARK! Finally, I got so fed up I woke up to find out what the hell his problem was, "What!" I tried to yell. But I couldn't. I couldn't speak because I couldn't breathe. I was suffocating on the phlegm in my lungs. It had clogged the air passage and there wasn't enough oxygen left in there to cough open a little air hole. I was literally choking to death.

Coming out of a deep sleep, out of a very vivid dream, choking to death ... no air. I couldn't breathe in or out, it was horrific. Finally, I rolled over off the bunk and slammed myself to the floor, chest first. It opened up enough of hole to allow a little bit of air to pass and I began coughing out the phlegm and gasping for life-saving air. It was close.

Make of it what you will, but I absolutely know what happened that night. My old buddy had come to me through space and time to save my life. Kokomo had saved my life, answering the question that has perplexed man for so long, do dogs have souls? No longer a question without answer, for me, at least.

All these years later, I still think about Kokomo, still regret leaving him waiting for my return. Maybe he got tired of waiting and came looking for me, romping through those endless forests trying to find his old friend, finally finding me on that Highpower row, saving my life and continuing on looking for that ultimate place of adventure where we could go exploring once again like the old days, searching for that special place where the woods won't end.

CHAPTER 12: OUT OF THE DARK

Pitiable human frailty,
Susceptible to the minor whims of a fragile ego
In our delirium we wander aimlessly,
Searching blindly for a doorway to lead us from the dark
Resolve weakened by a thousand self-inflicted wounds
Clinging to painful mementos of remembrance
Unwilling, unable to let go of the toxic guilt
The pollen of regret filters through the cracks
Of the dusty chambers of our mind
Pulling us back, refusing to let go
The winds of doubt bending the willows of hope
Blocking the light that might lead the way
Out of the darkness of despair.

- DRB

I guess you might be able to discern from the nature of that passage that I haven't always had the most optimistic view of the world. The truth is, for the greater portion of my life I was mired in the quicksand of depression and felt I really had no control over so much of life, that at times it seemed so difficult to rise above the circumstances I repeatedly found myself in.

And, in fact, I was right in that assessment. I was powerless because I was unaware of vast limitlessness that was available to me, to all of us.

The scientist, Sir James Jeans, wrote: " ... the universe shows evidence of a designing or controlling power that has something in common with our own individual minds."

It was only after finally falling so low that I felt I couldn't sink any lower that I turned inward, deep inside that vast chasm that seemed to produce nothing but pain and torture, that I began to discern there were greater powers at work than my own tiny ego-driven quest for personal satisfaction. By shutting down my own needs and finally 'listening' to the great void, I was able to begin to piece together the puzzle of existence.

A question I'd always had was, if there is a God, and He is responsible for everyone and everything, then why is there so much suffering in the world? The fallacy in the potential answer lies in the paradigm from which the question is posed. You see, it was my limited understanding of the nature of creation which led to the impossibility of a satisfying answer.

I was operating from an ignorant position, limited by my short-sighted perception. I was assuming that when anyone spoke of 'God' they meant the white-bearded anthropomorphic version attributing human shape and characteristics to 'Him'. And, honestly, there are a lot of individuals and even whole organization that believe that. This had always been a failing point, for me, in the conversation and question, "Does God Exist?"

And, there was the suffering issue. If somebody is looking out, then why all the hungry babies and war and hate and pain and destruction? And how the hell had I found myself at the tender age of 22, with nothing but bright potential ahead of me, waking up from an alcohol-induced walking blackout to discover the path of destruction I'd blazed, ruining everything?

Turns out 151 rum isn't the cure-all and answer and solution to life's travails. When it's mixed with Coca-Cola, you can't even taste the toxicity going down. I couldn't stand the thought of doing the time for the crime, not back then. Five years seemed like such a long stretch. Ah, the ignorance of youth. I ran.

This was before the Internet, there weren't any cell phones or computer-based Google maps and technology was fixated on Pong and VHS tapes. I think we had video back then, cutting edge stuff. I had run into an old convict while working some transient job in construction. You can't be a reporter anymore when you're on the run. He gave me game on getting new I.D. and I soaked it up like a greedy sponge. I needed fresh I.D., the one I'd been using since birth was worn out. First stop, the graveyard.

I can't express how morbid it is when you're wandering through the graveyard trying to find just the right dead person from which to build a new identity. And what's worse, you have to find a baby that died before they reached the age of one year. You see, back then, there were no death certificates filed for children that died before age one. When you're on the run and desperate for I.D., you can't let the somber unwholesomeness of the process prevent you from achieving your goal, however. You can't afford to think about the morality of the act, just focus on the prize.

Many cemeteries bury folks in chronological order. Meaning – if you want to find a body buried in the approximate year you were born, you go to that area of the graveyard where that year's unlucky folks are planted. Then you look for birth – death dates that are less than a year apart. Next stop, the public library, microfilm section. You go through the old newspapers from the days just following the baby's birth to find a birth notice. From there you can get the parent's names, birthing hospital and most important – the mother's maiden name. With this info you can go to the Hall of Records and tell them you lost all your I.D. and need a certified copy of your birth certificate.

With that golden ticket, a certified birth certificate, you can get a brand new driver's license, social security card, credit cards, everything. It's pristine I.D., no trail that leads anywhere. Since there's no death certificate filed, you're simply assuming that dead child's identity. It's real I.D. During the years I was on the run I obtained several new I.D.'s. I got pulled over by the police and had it run through their system, nothing. I did have a cop ask me once, "You've NEVER had a traffic ticket?" I was about twenty-eight years old. He seemed confused and impressed.

I fled Florida with all the speed and enthusiasm that youth provided, landing on the opposite coast as far away as I could get and still be in the continental U.S. At least, Los Angeles seemed as far away as I could get. Turns out, the best place to hide is in a very populated metropolis, you simply blend in with the crowd.

But you need money and/or contacts to live in L.A., and I had neither. I got tired of the temp jobs and trying to find something that would pay well enough to provide adequately; so finally I went to one of the private employment agencies on Wilshire Blvd. and told them, "Just send me on an interview to the best paying job you've got." It didn't matter what it was, I was intent on acing the interview. They had a listing for an accountant in a law firm in one of the downtown high rises and asked, "Do you have any accounting experience?"

"I've got a year of bookkeeping from high school."

Good enough. The agencies make a hefty commission for placing an applicant. The agent fixed me up with a fake prior job background and gave me a phone number that rang at her desk. I give the false reference and phone number and when they called to check my reference, she gave me a glowing report. I aced the interview, they called and got a great reference report, I start Monday.

It turned out this wasn't just some modest law firm, it was a law corporation with offices in L.A., Palos Verdes and Fresno. They had contracts with all the school districts and made huge bank billing and over-billing clients. The previous accountant was leaving and I was to take over all accounting operations immediately, "Could I do it?"

"Sure, why not?" I took all their books and ledgers and balance sheets and everything else to a legit accountant. I didn't have a clue how to do what was needed. In one night she showed me how to do debits and credits, billing, payroll, fiscal reports, balance sheets and the whole lot of it. I was in.

It was a lot of work, no lie. But as long as I kept at it consistently, it was doable. The firm had just moved the main office from Palos Verdes, a very rich and ritzy ocean view community, to downtown L.A., and as a result they had to move the finances to a downtown bank. Now, I had read like a hundred books on how to become a millionaire and one of the key points the informationals always referred to was 'O.P.M.'. Other people's money. They showed you how you make money by making it work for you. So, I called every major bank in town to come interview to see what they could do for the firm that would influence me to put the money in their bank. Every one of them wanted the account, they showed up like hungry lions to a meat buffet.

Crocker, Security Pacific, Bank of America, First Interstate ... their representatives, each and all, sitting in my office telling me what they could do for us. The thing was, all the partners to the law corporation were off doing whatever it is they do, none of it had much to do with law or corporating. I was left pretty much alone in the offices with the secretaries and receptionist and had the run of the place. They weren't even interested in the books as long as the bills were getting paid, the payroll was met and the billing was being done in a manner that kept the money flowing in.

I had complete control of the money and I wasn't shy in how I used it. I ended up using all the banks to our advantage. We had accounts in every one of them. When the head partner wanted to buy an over-priced vintage Mercedes, I used the corporate umbrella to finance the loan. I had law money invested in gold, diamonds, pharmaceuticals, commodities, stocks at the whim and discretion of a broker I met over the phone. I was floating loans to increase the appearance of net worth, buying real estate and padding the attorney's billing reports in a manner that doubled the gross income of the corporation. I was hiring temp office girls and assistants whenever I wanted or needed, taking trips to Vegas and New York at the drop of a hat, and siphoning off just enough of the filthy lucre to wet my beak and finance my own spendthrift lifestyle. It was a bizarre, crazy run, and I knew it couldn't last forever. Tax accounting and audits were inevitable, and I didn't plan on hanging around for any of that!

I sent the office girls and secretaries to the various banks with petty cash checks to cash every day for a week. Cashed in my own stocks and closed my personal accounts and prepared to bail. I packed everything of any value to me in my little sports car and headed up the coast. Good-bye L.A., hello whatever may come. I hadn't been gone two days before I was advised by someone I was keeping contact with that the F.B.I. had been to my place looking for me. They were on my trail and I hadn't even known it.

In San Francisco I got new I.D. and set up shop. Back to the employment agencies after I'd burned the bankroll up in Vegas. Somehow, I landed a sweet gig at Wells Fargo bank in their corporate offices. I knew I couldn't stay too long, even with new I.D. I hadn't secured a new social security card so I'd have to take off before tax season rolled around. I was making good money though so I wasn't that worried. Somehow, things always worked out.

The thing about being on the run is, you can never plant roots. You always have to be able to pick up and go without hesitation. When I bailed from L.A. I'd left everything behind in an instant, including a girl that I'd married – under one of the alias names, she literally had no idea who I was, of course, neither did I.

I didn't conceive of the terrible heartbreak and trauma I was causing and creating. I was just trying to survive and going on instinct, there was very little morality or spiritual guidance coming into play. I was just trying to stay ahead of the law and make a living. I wasn't trying to purposely hurt anyone, but if it came down to it and I had to go, I was gone.

That kind of mindset and lifestyle can really be exhausting, especially when you meet someone you really like or fall in love with … and they get pregnant. I'd been doing this for a few years, bouncing between L.A. and San Francisco and Las Vegas. I'd gotten used to it. When things were running well I'd store up bank and invest in items I could pawn or sell quickly when I needed money. Gold and jewelry is good, small, and easily liquidated.

Sometimes I'd have to find a girl to shack up with for a time, other times I'd meet more affluent women who didn't mind sharing the wealth. In either case it couldn't last, I couldn't afford to get tied down. Of course, the brain knows that, but even with so much at stake the heart has a mind of its own.

When I met Marivic everything changed for me. Suddenly, I no longer had the ability to pick up and go in an instant. I don't even know why, exactly. She wasn't the prettiest girl I'd ever known, or the most decent. In fact, she probably wasn't even that good of a match for me. But, these things are unexplainable and way beyond my ability to figure out. She got pregnant, the baby was amazing, I was in love and had a family now. So when the winds of change were blowing hints of danger in my direction, I ignored them.

They caught up with me in 1986. I was home in an apartment in Hollywood with Marivic and the baby. A former girlfriend I'd run out on had tracked Marivic's parents down and sent the authorities to them. She had run into us during some mad escape and memorized the address on the luggage tag on Marivic's suitcase. The parents were illegal immigrants and the cops leaned on them pretty heavy to get my location. I did four years, got out, tried to set up the nice family life by working myself to insanity eighteen hours a day.

All those years spent on the run, I could never run away from myself and I still hadn't figured anything out. I lacked coping mechanisms and self-awareness and emotional maturity. In 1993 I fell again. I lost Marivic and the kids, my career, my freedom, everything. After I lost the main case in 1998, I lost my physicality in the failed escape attempt.

Finally, finally I'd lost so much there wasn't anything else to lose. I'd hit rock bottom and there wasn't any place to go but up. I'd burned all my bridges so there wasn't anywhere to go but forward. There's something cleansing about total annihilation. Thank God I still had the meditation and some semblance of intellect. I couldn't move, but I could think, and I did a lot of that. After I figured out I couldn't meditate myself to death and I was too cowardly to use a razor blade, I opened myself up to whatever was out there and paid attention, for once. My studies brought me to the realization that 'I' was part of a greater energy. The energy from which everything had emerged. It wasn't a matter of 'me' doing this or that, and all my struggles were self-induced. If I'd just tap into that infinite power and be a harmonious part of it, everything would be fine.

I had to go through all this, to find out all that? Why so much turmoil and suffering to find that peaceful place that was right inside me all the time? The same question. If there is a God, why all the suffering in the world? Because without the suffering, without the strife and turmoil and adversity, man would never seek a higher awareness, a higher power and source. It's through our adversity we gain perspective and insight to evolve to our higher nature.

And God isn't that image of a man in a robe in the sky, looking down and judging every wrong turn ... but, rather, a great energy that's the combined energy of each and every one of us and all the planets and stars and the entire cosmos that has its own causes and effects and checks and balances.

When we discover this and set our minds right and find the goodness within, tap into that source energy and become a part of its harmonious embrace, THEN we discover the soul that connects each and all of us and allows us to be the person we were meant to be, and live the life we're capable of living. Whether we find it on a cliff overlooking the ocean, on a hilltop in the Himalayas, at a bus stop in Los Feliz or in a rat-infested cell in the L.A. County jail, it is there for us to discover.

> "The thoughts of the Soul are not ideas but creative powers ... the more the Soul lives in the light of the Spirit, 'turned towards' that which is above itself, the more creative it becomes."
>
> - Plotinus

As Gandhi so famously said, "Be the change you wish to make." Be the light that illuminates the dark. In a completely dark room, even the tiniest candle fills it with light. Look inside yourself, discover your soul, find that light that burns bright and is a part of the greater light of the world and the universe.

At the point where man meets the infinite, his higher nature and highest awareness, this is where he discovers that which is absolute, ineffable and inexhaustible This is where he transcends his own existence and finds that which is eternal. In this sense, belief in God becomes justifiable, even to the most staunch pragmatist.

In a scenario where we're striving to become better people, rehabilitate ourselves in order to become more benevolent, productive members of a society and worthy participants in interpersonal relationships, the higher consciousness that is available to all, that's within us all, is the connecting link to that which will bring us, each and all, out of the dark and finally into the light.

CHAPTER THIRTEEN: EVOLUTION

In a July 2015 *Rolling Stone Magazine* article, writer Tim Dickison points out that politicos, en masse, are falling all over themselves to secure a seat on the bandwagon bemoaning and criticizing the crass and blatant effects of over-sentencing and mass incarceration. Apparently, as campaigns ramp up for the 2016 presidential election political A and B listers such as Democratic front-runner Hillary Clinton, Republican Senator Ted Cruz, the Koch brothers of Koch Industries, financier George Soros, the ACLU, and most of the other near score of presidential contenders, have seen the light and are appalled and dismayed about the lives lost to insurmountable prison time.

Hallelujah and don't hold your breath. It's not going to last. When Hillary says, "It's time to end the era of mass incarceration!" Somehow, it's not a comfort to any of us who are stuffed in a dorm filled to the gills. Every time it rains the ceiling and walls leak buckets and the floors flood, the toilets are not only disgusting but leak and break down every week; the J-cats are barely coherent enough to use the things, anyway; the food is repugnant and healthcare questionable, at best. The formal complaint system is a joke – you file a complaint and it's denied or sent on an end-run all the way around constitutional rights. Many times, when we file Habeas

Corpus writs, they simply do not get a response. Jeez, they even kill prisoners for sport and there's no retribution, so are we really believing the rhetoric about ending mass incarceration?

It's just words. Words are easy, all you have to do is open your mouth and blow. Action is hard, that's why so often, there isn't any.

Prosecutors, private prison investors, guard and police unions, tough on crime judges and politicians – the individuals and groups that safeguard the American public and act as gatekeepers between 'us' and 'them', aren't listening to the cries of injustice. What's less politically incorrect than arguing for lighter sentences and being softer on crime? All it's going to take is one (more) parolee to go jihad on some law-abiding innocents and the argument for an end to the madness will cease. Again.

With prison population rising 500% over the past 40 years and the U.S. housing a quarter of the earth's prisoners while accounting for only 5% of its population, reform advocates insist there is something indefensible in our approach to criminal justice. One of every 87 white men are imprisoned, one in every 12 black men are jailed. The disparity is disturbing, but the numbers are unconscionable in either case.

Eighty billion dollars a year to keep Americans locked up, the average cost is $31,000 per head, rising as high as $60k in New York. The feds spend $8 billion with another $3.8 billion in state subsidies. Reagan's war on drugs, Anti-Drug Abuse Act of 1986 blew up the population and insured its rise into a major corporate and sociological entity. Three-strikes in 1994 piled on, ballooning the prison population and pouring billions in grants to states for new prison construction.

Cash poor states are now suffering the sugar rush of mass incarceration highs and unrestrained prison construction, waking up in a recession with a lethal spending hangover.

In California, non-violent 3-strikers are no longer imprisoned for life, after a 2012 voter's initiative, and Proposition 47 defelonized minor drug offenses and nonviolent property crime – all in order to reduce population levels and allow some semblance of sanity to the law. California's activism has reduce the state's incarcerated by 40,000 a year, saving millions annually.

All across the country incarceration is big business. One in every ten inmates are housed in for-profit corporate prisons. Financially distressed rural communities depend on local prisons for jobs like old factory and mill towns of the 20th century. Local TV ads proclaim, "If you don't have any felonies, have a high school diploma, or equivalent, and are a legal resident of the U.S. (I think they even mentioned, 'if you have a green-card') then you qualify to be a California Department of Corrections' guard. Enroll in training, now, financing available." Believe me, the bar is set quite low to be a prison guard. And, they're hiring!

Some of the guys did Internet checks on some of the medical staff here, many had suspended licenses or questionable documentation – still hired, still working. Apparently, qualifications are subjective. Show up with a document stating you attended medical school in Bulookookistan and you can start immediately. Hey, who am I to complain about questionable background checks to gain employment? Just being real, not all the cons are convicts.

If you've never been convicted of a crime, are you a criminal? Only our doctors know for sure. There's really no getting around the fact that prisons are an 'industry', and in capitalistic America, if it doesn't make money it doesn't make sense.

Forty years of tough on crime mentality got us here, how many years to get us back to sanity? Or, is there any going back? Have we gone too far to ever regain that idealistic innocence that was the post WWII baby-boom mentality? With TMZ and media at large glorifying fame and material gain, no matter how you get it, as the new ideal, will things ever be the same?

From Franklin Roosevelt's 'New Deal', to the Kardashian image of the 'New Ideal' where sex tapes are the road to success and influence, how can we even hope for hope? Or have we finally reached the precipice of the seventh level of hell and are trying to put a bow on it by glorifying the gore and garishness that our insatiable appetites have begat us?

You know what? I'm going to have to blame O.J. for all this. Yep, it was during that televised trial that everyone started to figure out that criminality could be exploited for financial gain. If the dang Chinese media was sending over their network coverage, it must have been valuable. I wouldn't be surprised if it was a network executive that set the whole thing up. "Juice, baby, here's the scenario. The ex-wife and her boy-toy are found brutally murdered, we cast you as the obvious culprit, evidence beyond guilt, then in a stirring plot-twist, find you 'Not Guilty'! The ratings will be off the hook! Of course, we'll have to kill the girl to give it that realistic twist. We suffer for our art."

Don't you get it, don't you see? Kim K. is O.J.'s old attorney and best friend's daughter; their reality show is simply a continuation of the reality show that was the trial of the century. The investors in that are the same money guys who invested in private corporate prisons. Cashing in on the criminality money cow! Is all this hard to believe? Is it any more difficult to believe that there are people doing life-sentences for crimes they didn't commit, or that teenagers come in with a year or two to do and end up with a life sentence behind having to stand up for themselves or for defending themselves during a riot or attack?

Before I got sent to Highpower, in L.A. County on the tiers with eight or twelve stuffed in a four-man cell, down the tier I'd hear, "Hold him down, homeboy!" And the muffled cries would continue on through the night.

Yeah, prison isn't supposed to be nice Well, mission accomplished.

I can tell you, for sure, it's not easy finding your humanity when so much inhumanity is going on around you, from every direction. People out there think whatever we get in here we have coming. Ninety-five percent of prisoners eventually get out. These guys who have been subjected to the worse conditions imaginable with little or no guidance or treatment, back on the streets, to do what? Be conscientious citizens with upstanding morals and decent, proper behavior with no anger or substance abuse issues. Is that realistic?

When a prisoner gets out with his $200 gate money, he's going to have to find a job and housing right away. If he doesn't have family the housing is going to be difficult. And getting a job with 'convict' listed as former occupation isn't going to help much. It's no wonder recidivism is in the high 80% range.

The purpose of this book is to open a prisoner's eyes to his own personal potential so he might be able to tap into that higher awareness in order to seize his humanity, become a more empathetic, expansive individual who can strive for a better life and uplift those around him.

The adversity we face inside may be just the impetus we need to propel us to search for our better nature. We HAVE to become better people, it is our evolutionary privilege and mission to improve as thinking, feeling human beings.

The last two nights on the nightly news they've been showing the explosion of a hazardous materials factory in China. The blasts left carnage and destruction for miles around. Burned out buildings, cars gutted and left in lots and on the roads, a war-zone effect reminiscent of some apocalyptic nightmare. The kind of scene you'd expect from a dystopian novel made into a movie. But, it's no movie, it's real.

How many nations now have the atomic bomb? U.S., Russia, France, England, Pakistan, India, North Korea, China, Israel ... off the top of my head, but how many more? Is it that far-fetched to believe they might be used, again, at some point? Making the Chinese factory explosion (if that's really what it was) a prophetic vision come to life.

Are citizens out there too busy with their own personal lives to strive for personal betterment that centers on soul awareness and spiritual growth? When they have the cars and houses and mistresses and pool boys and kids in college to stress over, is there any time left for personal improvement?

Is it the convict's job, then, to attempt and improve the world by first refining himself? A delusional and far-fetched idea ... perhaps. But if the normal citizen is too busy to find time for deep introspection, then who is it left to?

From your dorm in a California prison, from your cell in an Arkansas joint, from your chain on a Louisiana gang, from the row of death in Arizona ... the call rings out ... save yourself and save the world!

A few nights ago Keith Kakugawa and Woodrow Fitzhugh invited me to a Buddhist gathering during evening program. I've been pounding out ten pages a day in order to have this published in time for my board hearing next month and it's literally wearing me out physically and mentally. I was reluctant to pull myself off of my bunk and subject this diminished body to further wear by sitting up for the extra hour or two. But, as philosophy and mysticism teach, people arrive in our lives at just the right time to assist us on our journeys ... when we're in tune with source. As was the case that night.

In the midst of some of the most depressing conditions one might find, fences and razor-wire and walls and bars and hate and depression, here were seven guys who were making the effort at communally raising their consciousness to a level that would override the morass of dejectitude that envelopes this place, and others like it, to find that inner peace and calm and creative, kind, loving, beautiful, expanding, abundant, receptive center that we all have, that we can all find if we just look. I was glad and inspired to be among them.

After witnessing that gathering of enlightened souls, each and all open to a higher awareness, all striving to be better than they have been and in doing so, up-lifting each other and their community ... maybe it's not so outlandish or impossible to consider that we, the dregs of society, imprisoned due to behavior deemed hazardous to the safety and security of society, might be able to contribute to the advancement of humankind, after all.

With 95% of us going back out and into the world, it would be advisable that we, at least try to be of benefit, after all, it is our responsibility as humans.

No living creature in the kingdom of animals knows more than its immediate surroundings or cares for more that the sustenance of its immediate existence. It lives in an immense and varied universe but the fact is lost to its mentality and outside of its interest. To us, our instinctual animal nature.

Only when the evolving entity attains the stage of developed human being does this unconsciousness disappear. Then life takes on a larger meaning and the life-force becomes aware of itself, individualized, self-conscious. Only then does a higher purpose become possible and apparent.

As we become enlightened, so too do our objectives and goals. Our higher natures revealed, the limitlessness within reach, we head out into that great nothingness where everything is possible.

To fulfill our purpose on Earth, and find true peace of mind and an end to the restless, agitated, uncertainty of life; seek the divine within.

Evolution in a philosophical sense is not the same as materialistic evolution. With us it is simply the striving, through cyclical ebb and flow, for an even fuller expansion of our individual consciousness. However, the ego already possesses all such possibilities latently. Consequently, the whole process, although an ascending one, is really an unfolding one.

The ideas and understanding in a man's mind are hidden and unknown, until discovered. To whatever limit or limitlessness he is capable. At our very core we have an innate understanding of 'everything' and it awaits our searching and discovery. That's why, 'anything is possible'.

It is to this higher awareness, this higher nature I call you to quest. I have no doubts about your infinite nature and ability, now, you must be aware of it too.

D. Razor Babb

CHAPTER FOURTEEN: THE LAW OF ATTRACTION

"The Universal Mind is not only intelligence, but it is substance, and this substance is the attractive force which brings electrons together by the law of attraction so they form atoms; the atoms in turn are brought together by the same law and form molecules; molecules take objective forms and so we find that the law is the creative force behind every manifestation, not only of the atoms, but of worlds, of the Universe, of everything of which the imagination can form any conception."

– Charles Haanel (1866-1949)

Haanel was a successful businessman and the author of several books, all of which contained Haanel's own ideas and methods that he used to achieve greatness in his own life. His most famous work is <u>The Master Key System</u>, which provides twenty-four weekly lessons to achieve greatness, and is as popular today as it was when first published in 1912 – over a hundred years ago.

I find it particularly interesting that this type of teaching has been going on for so long and probably more to the point, what took me so long to find it?

Because everything is energy, and energy cannot be created or destroyed, just changed in form, this means, because you and I are pure energy, we will always be. Yes, even after death, the death of this body the energy moves on. You're an energy field inhabiting a body, and a part of a greater energy field that consists of 'everything'.

In Rhonda Byrne's, <u>The Secret</u>, Dr. John Hagelin, a world renowned physicist, educator and public policy expert, states: "Quantum mechanics confirms it. Quantum cosmology confirms it. The Universe essentially emerges from thought and all of this matter around us is just precipitated thought. Ultimately we are the source of the Universe and when we understand that power directly by experience, we can start to exercise our authority and begin to achieve more and more. Create anything. Know anything from within the field of our own consciousness, which ultimately is Universal consciousness that runs the Universe.

So depending upon how we use that power, positively or negatively, that's the kind of body in terms of health, that's the kind of environment we create. So we are the creators, not only of our own destiny. We are the creators of the Universe. So there's no limit, really, to human potential. It's the degree to which we recognize those deep dynamics and exercise them, the degree to which we harness our power. And that really has to do again with the level at which we think."

It is difficult to dispute the teachings of someone of such great accomplishment. Hagelin is saying that every possibility exists. We access this immenseness through imagination. All you have to do is hold your mind on the end result intended and imagine filling the need. Ask, feel, believe, receive. You hold everything in your consciousness.

You attract to you that which you focus on intently. Apparently, I think about disgusting, loud obnoxious a lot, because I sure get more than my share. But, I get a lot of nice things, as well. Especially since I became aware of this dynamic. Good things and people seem to be coming around more and more. And the bad stuff, not as much.

I've really had a time, moving to a dorm, with the noise and ill-mannered types. Remember, I've been down 22 years, mostly in a cell, sixteen years of it single-celled, so dorm living is a huge change. Also, I've done all this time not knowing I'd have a shot at parole. So, my attitude has been, if it comes down to it, if you disrespect me enough, it's going down. I've worked on this, but somehow I tend to attract loud, obnoxious people. Well, becoming aware of the attractor principles, that you attract that which you are thinking of (with feeling), I started to realize I was attracting whatever was coming to me through my intense dislike of it. Because I hated it so much, I was attracting it. I've worked on it, I've been working on it … nothing good comes easily. But, I believe in the theory and actuality, and things are improving.

When you emit the perfect frequency of vibratory energy that's aligned with what you want, the perfect people, circumstances and events will be attracted to you and delivered. That's the law of attraction.

"Whether you think you can or think you can't, either way you're right."
– Henry Ford

There's no limit to what you can do when you believe in this principal.

After the fall during the escape attempt I was laid up in the jail hospital and pretty much couldn't move. After I got over the initial shock at having my body dismantled, and dragged myself up out of the hole of despair, I began focusing on what I 'could' do, instead of what I now couldn't do.

They don't give you a whole lot of time to lay there, either. Once the broken bones are set and you're safe to move, it's off to state prison. I'd done a previous term so I had some idea of what I was facing, but facing it from a wheelchair is something different. Suddenly, guys who would never have looked cross-eyed at me were bad asses. If you can't fight then some dudes think they can say any old thing. It took some really deep introspection and studying and growing in order to overcome that. The difficult thing is, 'you' are the one who has to do the growing. By 'you', I mean, in this case, 'me'.

Luckily, I came across Dr. Wayne Dyer's PBS lecture on The Power of Intention. Wherein he talks about source energy, interconnectedness, meditation, the seven faces of intention: creative, kind, loving, beautiful, expanding, abundant and receptive. The principles I've been talking about this whole time. When I started to get past my own ego, I began to develop and the minor bull crap guys on the tier could toss out seemed trivial, for the most part. As a side note, I've been studying this stuff for years and years and still get caught up, occasionally, in the old ego-driven low energy pit. But, I also know I have way better energy and things to do than that whole mess, and I'd like to be able to say the same of you.

So when I got to state prison in 1999, and they wouldn't let me stay on the mainline (cos they's killa's up in ther', fool, and they probably saved my life) I had to look around and see what kind of job or hustle was available due to the fact I didn't have anybody on the outside to assist, and I was used to providing for myself. My old dad was there, but he was in pretty bad shape dealing with medical issues. Last term I was Program Administrator's Special Project's Clerk, they actually made that position up for me. In county, before Highpower, I was staff barber, so I was used to the good jobs with the top pay numbers. But, now I'm in a wheelchair, so what job can I get?

I litigated handicapped issues for three years, getting shower benches, caregivers and ADA inmates on the inmate counsel. After being pro-per I was still in the litigation mode. I figured I worked so hard at that that they'd give me the lead ADA (Americans with Disabilities Act) position with a pay number. At the last minute they gave it to somebody else, somebody who wasn't even ADA. I'd worked on handicapped issues for three whole years and was pretty burned up over that. And, they decided the best job for me was wiping tables in the dayroom, no pay.

That's when I quit litigating and started writing, I mean writing for real. I started writing and publishing *The Corcoran Sun* yard paper right out of my cell and distributing it on the yard, Then got it on other yards and into other prisons. I wrote advertisers to try and get them paying for ads and got a few bites. Enough to buy suppliers and some canteen. I started writing Icicle Bill, the first novel, the same day I started writing *The Corcoran Sun*. I put Icicle Bill in as an episodic drama series.

This is all while reading The Power of Intention where Dyer is telling us about tapping into that source energy and that anything is possible. I really started getting into it. I read everything I could on everything having to do with higher awareness, spirituality, philosophy, self-help, and all the great literature I could in order to improve my writing skills. Dickens, Hemingway, Hugo, Dumas, Tolstoy, Bronte, Austen, anything and everything anyone had or I could find at the library. As a side note, the best books I've read in the literary sense are <u>Les Miserables</u> by Victor Hugo, and <u>The Color Purple</u>, by Alice Walker. On the spirituality, self-help side, <u>The Power of Intention</u> by Wayne Dyer, <u>Autobiography of a Yogi</u>, Paramahansa Yogananda, and <u>Perspectives</u> by Paul Brunton. <u>The Alchemist</u>, by Paulo Coelho is right up there, as well.

I submitted articles to magazines and entered contests, got a few published and a few contest wins. One of *The Sun* advertisers, *Inmate Classified*, has a pretty widely read website and Webmaster J offered to post <u>Icicle Bill</u> on there as a series. Then he took the second one, <u>Goodbye Natalie</u> and posted that. We had more than 10,000 hits on <u>Goodbye Natalie.</u> Out of all my books, that's everyone's favorite, so far. A minor publisher saw my <u>Icicle Bill</u> and offered to publish it in paperback at the same time another small publisher was making a similar offer. Webmaster J wanted to keep it as an on-line series, but since I'm in prison, all we get is paperbacks, so I chose to publish through one of the independents.

A couple of PEN contest wins, publishing offers, *The Sun* beginning to go national, I thought that was it! I thought <u>Icicle Bill</u> would go to the top of the best seller lists and into movie production ... my ticket out.

Not so fast, fool, the universe isn't done with you. I still had some growth to do. The little publisher didn't really have a marketing scheme, the outside publisher that took *The Sun* national wanted to do it their own way and started putting girlie shots and pimp stories in there, Webmaster J was mad because I went with the paperbacks ... but, it was all good, the best advice I ever got concerning writing was from Webmaster J when he told me, "Just keep writing."

And that's what I did. After <u>Icicle Bill</u> and <u>Goodbye Natalie,</u> came <u>Last Lockdown</u>, <u>Cherry Moon</u>, <u>Where the Woods Won't End</u>, <u>Outcast</u> ... I was building my library. I got yanked out of the cell and into a dorm and ran into a guy, Ron Gregg, who was at the writing table every day and needed some help. We finished the 475 page novel, <u>Savages, The Beginning</u>, the day before I began writing this one. In between I wrote <u>Babb's Writer's Workshop</u>, a how to write and publish from inside series. <u>American Prisoner</u> is planned as a series and my new publisher, LWL Enterprises, Inc., is the kind of publisher I've only hoped and dreamed of here-to-fore. Letter perfect, conscientious to a fault, inspiring, fast and thorough.

It's 40 days until my Board hearing, and <u>American Prisoner</u> will be on the table for the hearing. Keith will get it out over the Internet and my belief is this will be the one that's most widely distributed ... a prisoner's self-help and personal rehabilitation guide. I never saw that coming. Even during the writing of this, the usual things that get in the way: running out of paper, costly ribbons, typewriters breaking down, copying, mailing, all kinds of distractions that prevent productivity ... all mysteriously, these issues every one – overcome.

Paper, supplies, copying, Keith comes through. Typewriter blows up, Ron's got the back-up and Doc's on the repair. Ribbons running low, somehow they show up. Spirit's in need of a lift, Woody pulls me up. Even with only a short time to get these pages into digital format and uploaded, my sister, Leah comes through while in the midst of a full-time consulting gig that only leaves her 36 hours per week down time, (minus sleep and travel). The universe is conspiring to assist. We're all in tune with source energy and it's flowing.

We are all connected, we are all one.

"The Universe is the Universal supply and supplier of everything. Everything comes from the Universe, and is delivered to you through people, circumstances and events, by the law of attraction. Think of the law of attraction as the law of supply. It is the law that enables you to draw from the infinite supply. When you emit the perfect frequency of what you want, the perfect people, circumstances, and events will be attracted to you and delivered!"

– Rhonda Byrne in <u>The Secret</u>

D. Razor Babb

CHAPTER FIFTEEN: THE GOLDEN PONY

A fair time ago there was a little boy growing up in a small farming community nestled in the hills of northern Missouri. Every Sunday the family would gather at the grandparents' place for dinner, and the boy would listen to the adults talk. Inevitably, the conversation would wind its way to the point of someone pointing out that this fellow or that had found his way into some form of difficulty because he didn't have any horse sense. The term 'horse sense' kept popping up week after week, year after year, and the little boy always wondered what it meant. But, in northern Missouri back in those days, little boys were seen and not heard, that was one thing the little boy knew for sure, so he dared not ask.

The grandparents lived way out in the country on a horse farm. Not a horse 'ranch' with beautiful thoroughbred racing or show horses, the grandfather dealt in farm horses. Back in those days folks still worked the fields with plow or draft horses. One day the grandfather traded for a beautiful Palomino pony, the kind with the gold coat and blonde mane and tail, and the boy fell in love with that pony at first sight! From that moment on the boy was on the grandfather, "Lemme ride the pony! Please, let me ride Buttercup!"

Well, being soft-hearted as most grandparents are, one day the grandfather picked the little boy up and plopped him on the horse's back, granting his wish. No sooner had the boy's behind hit the pony's back it took off across the pasture, gaining speed fast. The boy barely had time to grab the horse's mane for dear life!

Now this was the last thing the boy had expected, the pony was so sweet looking and innocent and beautiful, who knew it had the heart of a stallion! But across the pasture they went, down and over the creek and up the rise galloping at full speed. The wind was blowing in the boy's face, tears were streaming out of his eyes – he was scared to death, but excited too.

The pasture was about a good two acres wide and fenced in with railroad ties planted deep in the ground for posts and barbed wire strung all around. And as they were coming up on the end of the field, the boy began to realize, the pony wasn't slowing down! Not only wasn't it slowing down, he seemed to be gaining momentum. The hooves of the little horse pounded the grassy pasture in a determined effort that the boy felt with every foot fall. Surely he thought, by the time we get to the end the pony will slow down, or turn ... he has to! He's trying to pull the pony's head to steer it from disaster, but it's difficult enough just hanging on, the horse isn't cooperating.

Faster and faster they go, up the plain, over the ridge, straight at the wire! He doesn't see it! We're going to crash! At the very last second before they hit, the boy jumps!

The grandfather has been running after the pair across the pasture, and finally, out of breath, he catches up. The boy has rolled over and over in the grass and is lying there, stunned. The grandfather reaches him and asks, "Are you okay?"

The boy looks up, "Yeah, I'm okay."

The grandfather asks, "Why'd you jump?"

The boy doesn't quite understand the question, it should have been obvious, he exclaims, "He was gonna hit the fence!"

The grandfather shakes his head and grins a toothless smile, looking down at the boy, then over at the pony. This causes the boy to look over at the pony, who is standing by the fence, looking back at the boy.

The grandfather says, "That pony wasn't gonna run into the fence, that pony has horse sense, he has more sense than you do!"

From that moment on he finally knew what horse sense was, plain old common sense … as much sense as a horse has got.

* * *

That was the story I told the jury in the hacksaw blade pro-per case right before the ADA told her story about being in law school, right before they went to deliberate. When I was telling the story and we were riding across the pasture on the pony's back, I stole a glance over at them They were rocking in their chairs, wind in their face, riding the pony right along with me.

There's something I forgot to mention about the case. My defense was that after a riot broke out at court in the holding cell we all grabbed our property up before they dragged us out and I must have picked up the wrong legal folder – the one with the hacksaw blade hidden inside. And how this wasn't the 1930's when guys got hacksaw blades baked into a cake and sawed their way out, who does that?

The closing argument had been split up over the weekend and I did my final rebuttal close on Monday. I'd already told them about the ridiculousness of the cake scenario and that even considering anyone would try such a thing is preposterous. Well, over the weekend three guys had escaped from L.A. County jail's Supermax, using, you guessed it – a hacksaw blade! They'd had it sent in in a hollowed out bible. Of course. It was all over the news and in the papers. I felt my defense had just been torpedoed and before the jury came in I moved for a mistrial.

The ADA was positively beaming. I was sunk. The judge called each juror into the courtroom one by one, asking them if they had seen the news or read the paper over the weekend, did they know anything of any escape? Twelve jurors and an alternate, each and every one had not seen the news and had not read the paper. They hadn't heard a thing about any escape and if they did they assured the judge they wouldn't let it influence their decision. Motion denied.

What are the chances thirteen people who are sitting on a case that centers around escape didn't see or hear that news report? Didn't read a paper? Didn't catch wind of it when they entered the courthouse? About the same chance a pro-per had in winning a case before a jury I'd wager.

So I told them the pony story and told them that's what I wanted them to use when deciding this case. Horse sense, common sense to see that the ADA couldn't prove her case because she didn't have a case. That she would have never had to use lies and deceit if what she said was true. It's just common sense.

The legendary defense attorney Gerry Spence wrote in his book, <u>How to Argue and Win Every Time</u> that a jury thinks with its heart, and not with its head. And if they like you, they don't want to convict you. That's a good thing, because thinking back on it now, if they'd have used their common sense I think they would have figured out that it was my hacksaw blade.

When they came back with that 'Not Guilty' it was one of the highlights of my life, an inspiring moment and certainly one I'll never forget. I'll also never forget the extreme level of interconnectedness I felt with everyone in the courtroom. Judge, jury, prosecutor, witnesses, bailiff, audience. I hope you too have similar amazing experiences in your life.

I would ask you, as I asked the jury, in deciding the course of your life, as you're building a brand new history beginning from this day forth, to utilize horse sense, common sense, in deciding the day-to-day choices of how your life will be. It's all up to you. Hang onto the mane or reins and ride it out, or jump off at the last possible moment ... only you can decide what's best for you.

One thing I learned in that courtroom in Pasadena, everybody wants a pony. Yours is out there, waiting for you.

CHAPTER SIXTEEN: AMERICAN PRISONER

You may be, as I certainly am, one of the 2.5 million American Prisoners incarcerated in the United States. I don't know if that number includes those on probation and parole, or how exact the statistics play out after all the equations are quantified and calculated. Whatever the actual number is, it's a lot. Some of us deserve the time, some don't. Ironically, I know I would never have become the man I am today without doing the time, without the tragic losses, without the adversity.

Even the hell I went through age four to thirteen wasn't wasted. If I learned to not fear a grown man five times my size then some dead-eyed convict standing eye-to-eye ain't gonna faze me. And if the love of my life decides she's better off going her own way, well, I didn't own her to begin with. The kids, I intend on getting out and getting in touch, now that I'm someone I wouldn't mind them knowing.

When I was staring up at the clear blue open sky after falling sixty feet from the top of the L.A. County Jail, I breathed free air for the first time in a long time, and for that brief moment I was free. I'd made it out, escaped the confines of stone and steel and paid a hefty price for the fleeting freedom.

Since that time the things I've discovered, the people I've met, the circumstances I've encountered have all added to the rich texture of a life lived to the fullest. Even as I lived these past 22 years incarcerated, what I've found is so much greater than anything I lost. Through inner searching and elevated awareness and connection to source and soul I know I've never been more free and more certain of the vast limitlessness of the possibilities in life.

"Stone walls do not a prison make, nor iron bars a cage."
— Richard Lovelace (1618 – 1657)

Any American Prisoner, any person no matter where they are can live a peaceful contented, satisfying life full of success, love, creativity, kindness, beauty, abundance, if they are receptive to all that's available to them. Beyond and above the cages which impound us in self-imposed confinement we can find and live that wonderful life – the one we all deserve to live.

*

OTHER BOOKS BY D. RAZOR BABB

Icicle Bill

Goodbye Natalie

Last Lockdown

Cherry Moon

Where the Woods Won't End

Outcast

Savages (w/Ron Gregg)

Babb's Writers' Workshop

www.ingramcontent.com/pod-product-compliance
Lightning Source LLC
Chambersburg PA
CBHW061947070426
42450CB00007BA/1081